Why Trump Won

To Christine

[signature]

Why Trump Won

AND WHY HE WILL WIN
AGAIN IN 2020

Mitchell Steven Morrison

Copyright © 2017 Mitchell Steven Morrison
All Rights Reserved

ISBN: 1974588084
ISBN 13: 9781974588084

Acknowledgments

THIS BOOK IS DEDICATED TO my family. They bless me with the reality that nothing is more important than family: my children, Kaylen and Reed; my sister, Rebecca, and brother, David; my mom, Sophie, and dad, Fred Curly; my son-in-law, CJ, and soon to be daughter-in-law, Laura; and the grandchildren, Kapri and Kennedy. Lastly my wife, Bonnie, who has seen and experienced the highs, the lows, the bold, the brave, the longing, the lost, and the found. I also dedicate this book to very talented friends: Nick Yocca Jr. Esq., Cynthia Steadleman, and Malcolm O'Donnell, I give special thanks to the University of Southern California School of Journalism, USC Football, USC Rugby, Washington D.C. Rugby Club, Santa Monica Rugby Club, Delta Tau Delta Fraternity, Trojan Football Alumni Club, and Pastor Gene Molway, one of the greatest men I have ever known. Some of the proceeds from this book will be donated to the Financial Literacy Project, a nonprofit tax-exempt organization that teaches much-needed financial education at high schools and colleges (www.flproject.com).

Preface

I HAVE NEVER MET DONALD Trump. In fact, I've never met any Trumps before. I don't know his business partners or anyone who actually worked with him or his family members, and I don't know how he got the name "The Donald," his old nickname from days past. I am not qualified to be a biographer because I have never interviewed Donald Trump. I don't write about his past in this book, and I do not mention his upbringing or his early years in the real-estate business. I don't know how he made his billions. I mention a few things about his past in the book, but they are limited. I have never read *The Art of the Deal*. My research is based on library books, publications, the Internet, television, radio, and some inside information from Vladimir Putin. (Just kidding about Putin.) I did, in fact, study Putin's background, education, and career after I resigned from the Federal Bureau of Investigation. While I was employed by the bureau, I worked for a period of time in foreign counterintelligence on the SSG (Special Surveillance Group) squad. Back in the late 1970s and the 1980s, the former Soviet Union, or USSR, was very active in the "spy game." The FBI was also engaged and very active in trying to deter the former KGB, made up of Russia, East Germany, Bulgaria, and all the rest of the entire iron-curtain countries, including even Finland and Poland at the time. In my opinion and experience, espionage and hard-core spying was more prevalent back then than even today. I remember with all those other iron-curtain countries engaged, including Cuba, the operations were coming from everywhere. So this newer Russia is different, not like the previous USSR, which would routinely conduct intelligence gathering on a daily basis and around the clock. Deep mole operations, "singletons," "developed agents," "defectors in place," "dead drops," and "false flag recruiting" were all part of the USSR and former KGB and GRU spy game. However, that is a whole other book I will perhaps write one day. That being said, I want to someday have the opportunity to meet with Donald Trump. If writing this book gets me an audience with Mr. Trump, then that is a win for me. Perhaps—who knows?—I can even tell him a thing or two that may have an impact on him. I will say one thing: it will not be "fake news."

None of my family members or my close friends has asked me why I wrote a book about Donald J. Trump. I guess because he is the current president, number forty-five, of the United States of America; that would be a good reason. If you all remember the movie *Forrest Gump*, there was a scene where Forrest ran across the United States several times. In the movie he was asked, "What are you running for?"

Gump said, "I just felt like running." I guess you could say for me that "I just felt like writing."

I think sometimes the contents of a book last as long as the writer can still tell a story without running out of words. I was simply curious about Mr. Trump—sorry, I mean President Trump. I was interested in meeting Trump way before he became president. The reason for my wanting to meet him is to share ideas with a "captain of industry" like Trump. I have many ideas on how things can be changed in America to make it better. For example, I have always been surprised that a past president of the United States never appointed a cabinet member in charge of national philanthropy or charitable giving. There are numerous ways to make charitable giving more impactful, and certain tax laws could be used to create further incentives for businesses and whole industries to participate in these impactful ways. I would like to see specific human-aid projects carried out by businesses, and for the successful completion of the projects, the businesses would receive tax credits instead of just tax deductions.

I would like to see US history fully documented and officially recorded by the US government so the real truth about what has occurred over the years is not altered or changed. Leaving important events out of the equation or even changing the final result should not take place in our history books going forward. This, sadly, has been occurring in our public schools, and some important details are being left out. Most of the confederate statues are now torn down and some destroyed, but the ones that are not destroyed are no longer viewed by the public. This deconstruction of confederate statues erases important battles that were fought during the US Civil War. In an act of revenge, the Northern states' US Congress decided that punishment would be given to the confederates who fought against the Union. Some confederate generals were still placed under house arrest shortly after the war, and even Robert E. Lee, the famous general who led the confederate armies, was forced to live in a house that overlooks Arlington Cemetery, the largest military cemetery in the United States. He was mandated to live there rather than in the Alexandria, Virginia, home owned by his family. The Northern Congress of the United States wanted him to view the gravesites of those who died during the US Civil War.

I would like to see more vetting done on behalf of federal political offices and the candidates who are about to run for political office. Currently there are no official background checks on any candidates. The president of the United States, the vice-president, the US Senate, and the US House of Representatives have zero required background checks. I would like to have a federal law enforcement agency appointed to do background checks. In 241 years of our formation of the United States, there have been no background checks. Financial statements are required but no investigation of candidates' work history or personal information. The founding fathers created an outdated rule back when our country was being formulated. The wisdom of the times was that learned and educated men should do their own investigation and inform themselves with the qualifications and political views of the candidates. There are a couple things to point out. When the country was being formed as a republic, only men had a vote. In order to cast a vote, you had to be a landowner, and your family had to have roots in the community.

Background checks are required at all other government positions or agencies, including local, state, and federal positions, and they are required at McDonald's restaurants, Starbucks, Dunkin' Donuts, Burger King, Taco Bell, and all fast-food chains. I would think it would be disturbing that our lawmakers and policy makers in the federal legislative branch have zero professional background checks. Is it prudent to pretend that everyone who runs for office is honorable in his or her past business or personal history, and that he or she has been truthful? President Obama could not produce an original birth certificate from the state of Hawaii. Somewhere an official agency of the United States should be able to absolutely verify the place of birth and official record of live birth. When it came to Obama's college records and attendance, it was never verified at Columbia University. The bigger story (fake or real) was that Obama entered Occidental college of Los Angeles California as a foreign student. He entered the college as Barry Soetoro, having taken his stepfather's name when they lived in Indonesia before moving to Hawaii. Ann Dunham, Barack's mother, married Soetoro after her divorce from Barak Obama Senior in 1964, three years after Barak was born.

If Obama entered classes as a foreign student, he would be committing fraud also punishable with a possible felony. It is not a felony to use a name change, but it is a felony to falsify information to get foreign student aid. The most amazing fact is this: if convicted of a felony in the past, that conviction would not keep a candidate out of the White House. A felony conviction does not stop a candidate from running or taking the office of the presidency or, for that matter, any other federal elected office. This includes vice-president, the US House, and the Senate. Qualifications are very narrow for POTUS; they include the following: born in the territory of the United States and thirty-five years of age.

President Trump is not in the clear with his background, either. Opponents of Trump have been skeptical about his past business dealings and what he owns that may conflict with his official duties under the presidency. Either way, without the vetting process, how does America really know about the credibility and qualifications that can be verified on behalf of a POTUS? The amazing fact is that the national and local news agencies become the de facto investigators in this process. MSM have taken on the duties and become the background-checking source. Leaving the background investigations up to the "nightly news" is very scary and perhaps a dangerous situation. This is reckless at a minimum and should not be the case. There are just too many inaccurate reports and remarkably low standards fostered by these untrained reporters who are employed at the news organizations.

The real people in the United States will decide the next election. Not doing anything to fix Obamacare or repeal it will hurt the Republicans in general, and their approval rating is at an all-time low—88 percent disapprove of their ability to govern the country. Only 12 percent approve of their job so far. These statistics won't hurt Trump. He has called out the Republicans and exposed their inability to govern. In places like Ohio, Trump is moving ahead to do something without Congress and the Senate. He is actually doing something that former President Obama did nothing about: Trump is taking the drug-addiction problem head on. He has developed a special commission to come up with solutions and provide important resources. Currently in the United States, ninety-one people die each day from opioid overdose or overreaction. In 2015, 257 million bottles of prescription opioids were given out by US doctors. In 2015, 52,404 people died; the complete 2016 statistics are not out from the CDC, but the first nine months were greater than 2015, so estimates are placed at over 55,000 for 2016. Four out of five heroin addicts state that their addiction began as a result of prescription drugs. Cracking down on doctors, giving doctors more education on prescription pain management, and providing clinics are all part of this program.

I hope I have made a solid attempt in this book to give some strong reasons why Trump has the edge to win again in 2020, and I hope I have articulated his "go forward" strategy during this current presidency. Critics may ask me: How can you write a book about Donald Trump when you have never even met the man? My answer is that I have met and spoken to the

American people who voted for Trump in many different places throughout the United States from all walks of life. I have traveled to every state in the United States and all its territories except Guam. I have worked for companies located in New York City, San Francisco, Dallas, Charlotte, Little Rock, Los Angeles, Pasadena, Newport Beach, Irvine, Beverly Hills, Columbus (Ohio), Washington DC, and Quantico.

I have lived in: California, Connecticut, Maryland, Montana, New York, Ohio, Virginia, Washington DC, and even Canada. I am not considered a world traveler, but I have visited over twenty-two different countries and territories: Antiqua, Australia, Austria, Barbados, Belgium, Brazil, British Virgin Islands, Canada, Costa Rica, England, France, Germany, Ireland, Italy, Martinique, Mexico, Monte Carlo, Netherlands, Scotland, Switzerland, Tahiti, Ukraine, Wales...

Traveling to many places and living and working in different cities is a good way to develop an open mind and to see why people have their attitudes. It can further enlighten you on why they develop certain personalities. But the real reason I wrote this book is that I speak to friends and business associates all over the country. These folks live in Lincoln, Nebraska; Hays, Kansas; Manchester, Missouri; Palatine, Illinois; Payson, Arizona; Greensburg, Pennsylvania; Midland, Texas; Oxford, Mississippi; Gastonia, North Carolina; Old Greenwich, Connecticut; Bozeman, Montana; Copper Canyon, Texas; and Key Largo, Florida, to name a few. These people and places are where the cross section of Americans live. These are the vital areas overlooked where the polls got it wrong, and they will continue to get it wrong next time around in 2020. In fact, it would not surprise me if Trump was down in the 2020 future election polls and even predicted to lose in 2020. The polls are slanted toward who the pollsters want to win. In almost all cases, those who work for the polling companies are registered Democrats and lean liberal. The bottom line: polls don't win elections. Candidates win elections, and the Democrats so far "ain't got nobody" to beat Trump at the ballot box this next time.

I have identified at least 101 reasons why Trump won and why he will win again in 2020. See if you can list all 101 of them. Hint: fifty of them are already listed in one of the upcoming chapters. Take the Trump challenge and the why-he-wins-again challenge. I am offering this book free to the first two hundred people who mail me their correct list of 101. The items on the list can be the following: names of people, places, events, history, campaign promises fulfilled, and accomplishments. Please mail me your confidential answers (I don't want your answers being circulated throughout the general population, Internet, or to others in e-mails). If your answers are correct, then I will refund your purchase cost of this book in full. Please mail it to me at 18872 MacArthur Blvd, first floor Irvine, California, USA 92612.

Contents

Acknowledgments v
Preface vii

Chapter 1   Trump Is Not Just a Person, He Is a Belief 1
Chapter 2   Trump Is a Man's Man and a New Yorker 11
Chapter 3   The Mainstream Media Helping Trump 24/7 Using
            "Fake News" 19
Chapter 4   Hollywood: Let Them Eat Cake Because They Are All Fake .. 29
Chapter 5   Churches: Captured, Converted, and Committed 41
Chapter 6   Camelot in the White House—Trump Family 52
Chapter 7   Russia, Russia, Russia: False, Fake, Scam? 69
Chapter 8   Nicknames Are How Trump Keeps Winning 82
Chapter 9   Radical Islam, North Korea, Terrorism 88
Chapter 10 Congress: Throw Them All Out and Lock the Door! 98
Chapter 11 The Border Wall 111
Chapter 12 The Clinton Legacy: "Time to Stop Thinking About
            Tomorrow" 119
Chapter 13 Who Will Run against Trump in 2020? 126
Chapter 14 What or Who Can Bring down Trump While Still in
            Office? 138
Chapter 15 Making America Great Again 155

Epilogue 197

CHAPTER 1

Trump Is Not Just a Person, He Is a Belief

TRUMP IS A THROWBACK TO the "good old days." Most people may not realize that Donald Trump does not even communicate via e-mail. Trump still calls people on the telephone and even expects a face-to-face meeting in most cases. In the good old days, that is what you did. It is a dire mistake to try to negotiate using only e-mail. Those who try to do it using the computer or their smartphone will fail miserably. Trump speaks in a language that was used forty years ago, when politically correct language did not exist. Instead, Trump has developed, and brought back from the good old days, his own language. That language is called "politically direct." Not all of us remember or experienced the good old days. These were also the bygone days when America used to be really great. That was an accurate statement about America particularly shortly after World War II. The era of the 1960s and 1970s was the "tune in, turn out, and turn on," years with hippies, flower children, and the great "freedom to speak up and be heard" years. The 1960s and the early 1970s were the real protest years. The 1980s were the "go-go years" when fun, glitz, and glamor really took shape. Remember Studio 54 in New York City? Some people may say the real "good old days" were between 1946, just after World War II, and 1966, just before the ramp-up of the Vietnam War. Some would argue that the good old days continued into the 1980s, when many large fortunes were made and the salaries of doctors, lawyers, investment bankers, professional sports players, actors, entertainers, and performers started to skyrocket. There was a fantastic movie that hit the big screen in 1973 called *American Graffiti*. George Lucas was the director, and Francis Ford Coppola was the producer. It was about a bunch of high-school kids and their last days in the hometown before some of them went off to college. The date of the movie was set for 1962. The 1964 Mustang had not been invented yet. Back then practically everything was affordable: gasoline was cheap, homes were cheap, movies were cheap, food was cheap, and college was under $700 per semester at a college like Stanford University—less than $1,000 per semester for any college in the United States at that time. The prosperity ratio for all of America was more even keel back then, and the difference between the "haves" and the "have-nots" was not as dramatic back then. This proof of inequality and the elite class lies in today's compensation of athletes, actors, recording artists, Wall Street investment bankers, CEOs, and Silicon Valley tech moguls. Any member of a professional sports team who plays regularly in either the NFL, NBA, NHL, MLB, or professional soccer is an automatic millionaire. Now the normal contract for the top players involves hundreds of millions of dollars. Those "good old days" that your father, mother, grandfather, or grandmother refers to are not known by this new generation. However, the older generation recites this "good old days" story to the younger generation all too often. The talk of "the good old days" may be at the core of the current resentment and ongoing distrust of elders by the younger generation. Respect should be given to the elders who lived this life story. However, the younger generation has also rejected this time period as better times that have gone by, I believe because they feel that the "good old days" are never to return. Or at least the things that happened and were available as good times are no longer going to return in the younger generation's lifetimes. The current environment is in a confused state by the young and also confusing to the old and the middle-aged. The same theme pops up: "Are we doing better or worse as Americans? And are we going in the right or wrong direction?" Trump created this "huge" thought. The thought is: "Wait and see; I can 'Make America Great Again.'" But will it happen? That is the question. If it does happen, then Trump can claim victory for now. The next question will be: Can Trump and his followers feel better about America's greatness movement and "Keep America Great?" Or can Trump just make Americans *feel* great again? That may be, by itself, the answer for the Donald J. Trump presidency and the Trump final legacy. Lucky for Trump, if that is the case, the belief takes over for the reality. So far there are a lot of Trump believers out there!

I begin this concept with a quote from Maya Angelou. Maya was a famous poet and civil rights activist back in the 1950s and 1960s in support of Dr. Martin Luther King. She died in 2014. Maya stated, "I've learned that people will forget what you said, people will forget what you did, but people will never forget how you made them feel." Trump's presidential campaign and his victory made many people feel good about America again and therefore have a greater patriotic belief. Of course not all the people got this feeling. Not all Americans have that good feeling today. The polls say around 50 percent of those who did not vote for Trump would say Trump makes them feel sick! For those who supported Trump, they did feel good, and his campaign slogan said it clearly: "Make America Great Again." This slogan made his supporters feel good about themselves, not just about Trump as a candidate for POTUS. Hillary Clinton, in contrast, did not have anybody feel anything. She did not have the correct campaign message. Her campaign slogan was "Stronger Together." What Americans want to believe in and feel is greatness. "Stronger Together" is an ineffective slogan. It does not make us feel good about ourselves or about our country. It implies that America is currently a weak nation, and it almost sends the message that something bad or negative is coming to America, and we must bind ourselves together to ward off the impending hard times ahead. The nation is divided, but the divide is between the perception of patriotism in America and the direction of what America is supposed to look like in the future. Most of us want to be patriots; we also want a better life for ourselves and our future generations. Many of us believe we are patriots. What does it mean to be patriotic? Must we all serve in the armed services? Must we serve in the peace corps? Should we dedicate our time and resources to the poor and underprivileged? What is a patriot, anyway? I hear this phrase all the time: "Thank you for your service." Then who should be thanked? Members of the armed forces, police, firemen, EMTs? How about thanking teachers, truckers, social workers, construction workers, farmers, butchers, and safety inspectors? We as Americans are going to find out much more about our patriotism over the next four years. I think we believe that patriotism is a belief in America as the idea and notion that we exist in a country that is "the land of the free and the home of the brave."

Looking at America is not as simple today as it was years back. For instance, violence has sprung up in different ways and from more unexpected factions of the US population. Politics with vastly different views are now the norm. Who would have heard of a sanctuary city back in the 1960s, 1970s, 1980s, or even the 1990s? It goes without saying there are large groups in the United States who are no longer backing the American flag, the Pledge of Allegiance, and "in God We Trust."

It goes without saying that the founding fathers were patriots. The founding fathers were "older, white, rich males." That is a fact. Older, rich, white males are now a target within many liberal circles and the younger generation. The older, wiser, and experienced white men are not revered today in America. The younger generation believes that this group set up American society in a way that the American Dream would dissolve about the time that their generation would inherit it. This is the dream to prosper and take advantage of health, wealth, and happiness. More and more the liberal media today are asking: Are they [older, white, rich men] not the enemy of society today and part of the main problem? Did they cause the racial divide in the United States and oppression of Blacks, Latinos, Asians, Muslims, and so on? Now, are these same men the ones who framed a constitution that allows gun ownership and the right to bear arms? Back when the Constitution was being formed and drafted, the men who drafted it were the elite class. In order to vote or discuss laws of the land, you had to be male and a landowner. Women were excluded from the process of forming the original laws of the Republic of the United States of America and were not allowed to vote until well over one hundred years after the formation of the United States Constitution. The due diligence on President Obama was not exercised by the American public—in fact, quite the opposite. Obama was such an unknown, which was to his advantage. His US Senate voting record had not been tenured long enough to be criticized by anyone, including his opponents, the skeptical Democrats, or the mainstream press.

Before the vote for POTUS in 2008, the idea of an African American actually taking residence in the White House became a nationwide fascination. It wasn't that Mr. Obama was the best equipped to be POTUS with his background. From an experience level as a community organizer, he was vastly underqualified. He prevailed because he could connect and message with the American people. Obama was a communicator, plain and simple, and the best to come along since William Jefferson Clinton. Obama had a stronger message than Bill Clinton throughout his campaign for POTUS. The message was "Hope and Change." The time had come; after the George Bush years, America needed change. Trump took some of his strategy from the Obama playbook but seeking a different audience and group of supporters. Obama did in fact make many Americans feel good when he ran for POTUS. He made blacks feel very good, and even many white liberals felt better about themselves that America had finally broken the "color barrier." Obama, like Trump, was "a belief" and not just another political candidate running for POTUS.

Obama's opponent, John McCain, really had no message. If he did, I challenge anyone to recall McCain's theme or his message to the American people leading up to the 2008 election. In fact, the new emergence of a distrust of "rich white males" began with Bush and carried over to McCain when he ran for president. McCain was also much older than Obama, so he would perhaps be the whole package of distrust. Older, rich, white males are now a target of certain liberals and the radical left. Wisdom tells us that vilifying the white male really does not accomplish anything positive and leads the country into further divide and even the dark ages. Some would call it reverse racism or age discrimination if the, rich, white, older males are labeled and asked to relinquish their standing in the modern-day world. If some of these men helped to create an advanced society with a better quality of life for all mankind, then why are they now disliked and no longer trusted? This does not make sense. When things don't make sense overall in society, that is the beginning of a decline in society. Some would consider it a breakdown of society. Americans need to call it like they see it. The Middle East is a mess. The Middle East is a total breakdown of society. Death, terror, poverty, the haves and the have-nots are the norm in the Middle East; it is not a balance that is acceptable. Over one-third of the world lives in poverty, and poverty is on the rise. The growth of world poverty is a very legitimate threat to the United States. But the growth of world poverty pales in comparison to what America would be like if one-third of all Americans were living in poverty in the USA. It would cause chaos, and uprisings would be the normal course of action. It is important for all Americans to recognize this balance between the rest of the world and our world here in the United States. The United States can only take so many drastic changes before the people will rise up.

If there is anything you can absolutely say about Trump, it is this: Trump walks the walk and doesn't just talk the talk. How did most Americans feel when, during his campaign days, he was performing at peak levels and exceeding all expectations compared to past POTUS candidates? Trump was appearing at four presidential rallies a day all over the United States over the last four weeks leading up to election day. This was a big contrast to Hillary, who was not even able to maintain at least one rally per day in the final run for office. By giving that extra effort for a victory, Trump made Americans also feel good about this effort. Actions do speak louder than words. Trump showed much more mental discipline than Hillary Clinton and a lot more energy. When someone shows up and is energized, it makes a difference to the audience hearing the message. It also sends a message that "I am coming to you strong and confident that I am going to change things for the benefit of all." Trump gave a message that the other candidates were not willing to give. Trump said that if you are in the middle class in America, things are not going well for you, and they will get worse. "Make America Great!" meant make things drastically better for the middle class. Trump was able to use mental imagery, also referred to as visualization. This is the process of visualizing success. This is how he did it. Most politicians, if they speak on a subject like immigration, will say. "What we need is immigration reform." But what does that really mean to us regular Americans? How does immigration reform help me or my family? This is where the normal or typical politician fails to deliver a meaningful message. This is where people get bored or just really tune out the politician who is speaking. The politician has made a statement with no solution and no defined direction that the people of the United States can count on. So now here come Donald Trump, and he says the following, "We are going to build a big beautiful wall across our southern border. This border wall will keep the bad people out of the USA, and Mexico is going to pay for it." This was genius on the part of Trump, but also it gave a message with mental imagery and visualization to actualize the wall being built. With the message spoken in this manner, Trump gave two benefits that the American people could understand clearly: the wall will make us safer, and it won't cost the US taxpayers any money because Mexico is paying for the wall.

It also has made most Americans curious: What will the wall look like? How tall will it be? Will the wall really keep people out of the United States? It really is time for the liberals to admit that Trump brought out more emotion and dynamics to the voters than Hillary. The liberals will continue to push back on Trump because he does not speak about protecting the social groups. Trump cares about the working men and women in America; he cares about military veterans; he cares about those who serve in hazardous jobs like police and firemen. Hillary backed Black Lives Matter, the LGBT community, Planned Parenthood, and importing hundreds of thousands of Syrian refugees to be allowed into the United States—and visas for all of them. Some people might say "Hillary, you backed the wrong horse!"—or she backed the wrong horses such as, Planned Parenthood, transgender bathrooms, Syrian refugees, Black Lives Matter.

DON'T BELIEVE THE POLLS; THEY ARE JUST A FAKE AS THE MEDIA
Who pays for all these public opinion polls? During the campaign season or during political races, the campaigns will pay for polling, and so will certain groups like the DNC or the RNC. But who pays for all the public opinion polling and surveys? Before we get to that answer, here are some facts. You roughly have the same chance of being called on as anyone in the United States if you own a telephone. However, the chances of you being contacted for a typical Pew Research Survey is about 1 in 154,000. That number is a little misleading; the figure is more like 1 in 50,000. The typical size of a poll is usually around 1,500 people, and if you divide the US population which is around 235 million the you get that number. Not everyone has a phone out of the 235,000 million, and many of those are too young or too old to give answers to a survey. If you are on the "do not call" list, you are not exempt from being called. Survey research is exempt from the Telemarketing Sales Rule, which was adopted by the Federal Trade Commission to protect consumers from harassment. Also, charities and fund-raising campaigns for charities are also exempt from the "do not call" rules. The pollsters are supposed to follow a code of ethics, but these are meaningless. The pollsters can ask any question they wish and in any manner that they wish. This means they can ask questions that are misleading in nature. Many polls target certain groups as opposed to getting a survey on the entire population of the United States. The legitimate pollsters use the RDD Random Digit Dial approach, but some also use targeted lists to get a targeted result. They also ask questions when they reach a household like, "I would like to speak to youngest male in the household or youngest female." Young people are more difficult to interview and often do not have a real interest in speaking or giving their correct opinion.

Not only are the polls inaccurate, they are also manipulated. Many of the of the opinion polls are conducted by the mainstream media—NBC, CBS, ABC, MSNBC, CNN, and so on—and they are looking for a specific agenda or carry a message. In other words, they are using the polls to form or push a message that is either positive for someone or negative toward someone. For instance, they want Americans to believe that President Trump is to be viewed as untrustworthy. I will give an example.

The poll may ask who is more trustworthy, Donald Trump or Barack Obama? I would guess that in this poll Obama may get a 60 percent to 65 percent trustworthy and Trump may get a 35 percent trustworthy. But the reason is who they survey and how they ask the question. The MSM has gone on a constant campaign to discredit Trump, and they always bring up the Russia story every single day. It is always mentioned at least once a day. But in reality, it is Obama who has lied and misled the American public.

Obama said, "If you like your doctor you can keep your doctor." He said, "The Benghazi attack was caused by an internet video." He also said, "ISIS is just the JV team." I could go on and there are quite a few others that were just fabrications or lies by Obama. Yet the media is pushing a story over and over again, and they use the fake polls to back up the claim. They also say Trump has the lowest approval rating of any of the past five presidents. They get that result because they are not polling registered voters. Registered voter opinion is where it counts. But all this fake polling is still dangerous to someone like Trump because after a long period of time, when the people read or hear about all these low approval numbers, then they start to wonder: Did I make the right choice when I voted for Trump?

We must all have a belief today. Does it matter as a citizen what I believe today? Many of us ask: How can I put a dent in all the issues facing Americans today? If I do make a difference, who will know, who will care? This is a specific question by many people with good hearts. Sometimes what we see and hear from our leaders is the "happiness prevention team." The Holy Bible has a passage that seems disturbing but may also give us the answer to these questions.

Meaningless! Meaningless! Says the teacher.
Utterly meaningless, everything is meaningless.

> What does a man gain from all his labor at which
> he toils under the sun? Generations come and
> generations go, but the earth remains forever.
> The sun rises and the sun sets and hurries back
> to where it rises. What has been will be again.
> What has been done will be done again.
> There is nothing new under the sun. Is there
> anything of which one can say, "Look! This is
> something new." It was here already, long ago,
> it was here before our time. (Ecclesiastes 1:2–10)

The bible says that "all things are wearisome, more than one can say." Trump will have his days in the jungle of politics and have to put up with backstabbers all around him, but the belief is he will win with the people, and that is what will make the final positive outcome. The poor, the people in the ghettos living at or below the poverty line, will wonder if Trump is a modern-day Robin Hood—or is he just "Robbin' the Hood"? Only time can tell whether he makes a valiant effort to beat crime, poverty, high dropout rates in education, and high unemployment in the worst inner cities. Don't count on Congress or the Senate helping him out. Both houses have shown themselves to be true cowards and only looking for votes or to get re-elected. It is truly a shame that Trump will have to go this alone, with only a handful of patriots at his side. In the words of Sherlock Holmes, "The game is afoot."

CHAPTER 2

Trump Is a Man's Man and a New Yorker

IF YOU NOT SEEN "THE Honey Badger" on Youtube.com, then the next sentence in this paragraph will not make as much sense to you. Donald Trump is "The Honey Badger." The honey badger is a badger the size of a medium-sized dog. It lives in Africa and is a real animal. It is known for its ferocity and "pound-for-pound" awesome, predatory, aggressive behavior. It loves to hunt the king cobra, a highly poisonous snake, and other, larger animals—some very dangerous. The honey badger is intimidated by no one and seems to always control the situation. In the video, the honey badger eats a king cobra that is still alive. During the battle with the snake, the honey badger gets bitten several times and injected with the cobra's venom. The venom takes effect after the honey badger kills and eats the snake, but instead of dying, which would most certainly occur in a normal human being and most other species, the honey badger just falls asleep. It wakes up hours later, ready to continue eating the snake to finish off the meal and wreak havoc again. The narrator of the video sequence is quite entertaining and funny; he does an excellent job. He continues to call the honey badger "nasty and the honey badger just doesn't give a shit!" he states in the voice-over dialogue over and over, creating the funny effect for the viewer.

I have never lived in Queens, New York. I drive though there often going to downtown Manhattan. I am told you have to be tough to make it there in

Queens. It is a survival of the fittest–type attitude in Queens. Men and women from Queens are real New Yorkers with the attitude of "get out of my way or get run over." This environment would have been the foundation to build Trump's personality. He needs confrontation in his daily life; all the signs and manners points to this. Queens is the largest borough in New York and the most ethnically diverse. Established before the 1770s, it was the East Coast melting pot population wise. Trump grew up in Jamaica Estates the wealthy part of Queens, but this only made Donald Trump have an attitude, because he was called a rich kid. In the 1960s being called a rich kid was an insult. It kind of meant you were a sissy, and you did not know the mean streets like everyone else around the neighborhood. In the Queens neighborhoods, there were the Archie Bunker types who had the slang derogatory names for the ethnic groups. There were Kikes for the Jews, spicks for Puerto Ricans, waps or woops for the Italians, niggers for the Blacks, chinks for the Chinese, nips for the Japanese, Arabs were camel jockeys, Mexicans were beaners or wetbacks, and the Irish were called micks. The movie *West Side Story* was about a fictional Upper West Side Manhattan neighborhood in 1961. At the time the Queens neighborhoods would have been more accurate in the movie musical. Two gangs got into a fight, also called a rumble. The movie was about race relations and sticking with your own kind and not mixing with other nationalities. It was a Romeo and Juliet theme with a tragedy at the end of the movie.

One gang was called the Sharks, all young adults from Puerto Rico, and then there were the Jets, who were a mix of Italian and Irish street youths. Trump was not in a gang because of his strict upbringing. Trump actually went to military school out of the area. But he would come home for visits with his family, and he spent time in the Queens neighborhood. Trump experienced those confrontations—maybe not firsthand, but he knew about the streets, and it had influence on him about the streets. It would be a strong basis of his personality and attitude—that he was never going to be called a sissy or a rich kid, because that was not cool with the kids from the streets of Queens. For that matter, being called a rich kid was not cool anywhere in America in the 1950s and 1960s.

"I'll take Manhattan." I know that is a lyric in a song somewhere. I can't recall the matching song at this time. For a true New Yorker, they love it—every part of it. For all of the people who live in Manhattan or have visited Manhattan, you feel the high energy and the hustle and bustle of the city. It hits you in the face and resonates throughout your body. You walk faster in Manhattan, you talk faster, you think faster, and you get more aggressive with people. That is the attitude of the people living and working there and the way the entire city operates. It is a fast-paced lifestyle and no nonsense when it comes to being direct with everyone you encounter. No time for nice manners in NYC. So Imagine living and working there your entire adult life. Enter Donald J. Trump. He has lived and at least worked in Manhattan his entire adult life. True New Yorkers do not change their stripes when they leave the city or meet with other not from there. Trump will never change his personality, and that is why he is Trump.

Trump is not and will never be the normal politician. The normal or typical politician running for any office, but especially POTUS, and not from Queens and opposite of the honey badger will seek popularity first and foremost. To get elected first and to be popular is more important than to stand on principles. The normal politician will also seek the highest approval ratings possible. The typical political candidate does "give a shit," unlike a honey badger. The professional politician engages in a strategy to get high approval ratings and to agree alongside with the mainstream thought or seek to support the most popular opinions. "Go along to get along," or more accurately, "go along to get elected." The professional politicians will study and measure, with their teams of advisers, the impact of public polls to see what the public is thinking and what are the trends in America. As they take this popular path, many of them end up winning an election. Yet because of their noncommitment or middle-of-the-road attitude, the end result is that they get very little accomplished while in office. The other hidden, shocking revelation that they most likely will ultimately learn during their career in politics is that those who never take a stand are no longer trusted by the voters. They are no longer trusted, yet they often still continue out of habit and campaign advice. Many of them don't realize this trust is slowly slipping away the longer they are professionally vague and never take a stand.

Trump is a tweeter. He is on Twitter a least once a day, and at his best or worst, he tweets during the night even more so. The media does not get it. They, the MSM, are always going to lose when it comes to insulting Trump. Trump, when he gets insulted or is the target of a "media hit piece," will hit back. He will not take insults lying down or let them get away with insults. Ice water in his veins. The critics, who describe Trump as a "thin-skinned" individual and not able to handle critics' comments or editorials, have made a miscalculation. Trump loves this kind of altercation and sees it as hand-to-hand combat. He handles the media like the "Gong Show." In the Gong Show, if your act is not worthy, then you get booted off the show. Trump handles the media in the same fashion. If you ask him a question that is "not worthy," then you will be dismissed. Don't get me wrong, Trump is the least evasive and most transparent president in the last sixty years. Ask him a direct question, and he will give you a direct answer. It is when reporters have an insinuation or a negative remark based on false reporting or just fake news that Trump shuts them down. He does not hesitate to shut them down.

Trump is the most direct of all the presidents of the United States any of us can recall or remember. It is difficult to judge Trump against, Teddy Roosevelt, George Washington, Abraham Lincoln, because none of those past presidents ever experienced or appeared on live television. Something tells me that all of them would consider Trump brash, to say the least.

Most people equate Trump's fame and notoriety with the popular television show *The Apprentice*. Trump had high ratings for the show, and it was produced by Mark Barnett, the creator of CBS's *Survivor* series. Mark Barnett is a giant in the field of network television, arguably the best in the business. However, the real career and success that Trump mastered is the "dog-eat-dog" world of commercial real estate, mainly in New York City. That competition does not get any tougher. The toughest businessmen in the world build, develop, buy, and sell real estate in New York city. Miami is not far behind, and some of Trump's real-estate projects are now US landmarks, like a recent Chicago high-rise and the conversion of the old post office building on Pennsylvania Avenue in Washington, DC, into a luxury hotel property.

Trump has a huge ego, no question about it, and in his own words "Huge!" But he can also be deceptive and defer his large ego at times with his comments. More often than not, people do not pick up on that part of his personality and his communication skills. If you are the kind of person who does not like Trump, then he will most likely rub you the wrong way and annoy you when he speaks. Furthermore, you may detest his manner of communication. But whether you like him or hate him, he is extremely effective in one area. You can absolutely understand what he is saying. He speaks in simple English and does not attempt to "flower up" his speech. This is often overlooked by the media. The MSM does not appreciate his ability to communicate with all Americans and speak "to them" and not just speak "at them." Most politicians just don't get that part of what is appreciated by the American public. They want to hear direct words and phrases. Americans are tired of slogans, rhetoric, and tired old sayings that the speech writers keep coming up with over and over again. Examples like "At the end of the day," "Change we can believe in," "When they go low, we go high," "Russian collusion," "People are going to die," referring to the repeal of Obamacare, and of course the best one of all time, "Don't switch Dicks in the middle of a screw. Vote for Nixon in '72."

Potential detractors or declared opponents of Trump, such as elected congressmen, senators, government bureaucrats, lobbyists, foreign leaders, and reporters do not stand a chance against Trump. Trump is battle tested and battle hardened. Trump's real-estate experience gives the businessman Trump the edge over reporters, lawyers, bureaucrats, and entertainers. He has had to negotiate deals where millions are made or lost during these negotiations. Empires can be on the line, and fortunes are made or lost. The stakes are very high in all these cases, and those who have not been in that arena will fail against Trump. Remember when Trump said during his campaign, "You, those who support me, are going to get so tired of winning"?

Trump does not dodge the facts. He does lose his patience when it comes to opinions or the obvious negative agenda thrown at him. A recent Harvard study revealed that 94 percent of the news stories are negative to Trump. This negative coverage is unprecedented in all history of network television coverage and print organizations, such as *WAPO*, *New York Times*, *Los Angeles Times*, and so on. With all the negative thrown at Trump, he still takes it. He can take the criticizing, which is a strength that Americans can actually admire, and it keeps the belief in his resolve at the forefront.

Trump will call things like he sees them, and he has the will to go forward with a controversy or a subject and take it head on. The dramatic example of this is, calling out illegal voting in America and calling it "a rigged system." Of course he has been vilified by the liberals and the MSM when they come out a say, "how can you believe this great country of ours could have cheated in the elections?"

Trump continued to question voter fraud along with whether or not he lost the popular vote to Hillary Clinton. This subject is now coming to a head, and Trump has hit the nail on the head. There is voter fraud in America, and the proof is coming to light. Los Angeles county, California, just admitted in August of 2017 that the number of registered voter are at 144 percent of resident citizens of voting age. This is an incredible statistic and was confirmed by Los Angeles County officials. The Election Integrity Project California (EIPC) has come up with a list of eleven California counties that have more register voters than voting-age citizens. The nonpartisan EIPC has sent in the National Voter Registration Act (NVRA) section 8 notice of violation letter to California Secretary of State, Alex Padilla. The letter complaint has very specific information on voter abuse. It is quoted as saying," Eleven (11) counties in the state of California have more registered voters than citizens of voting age population (CVAP) calculated by the US Census Bureau's 2011–2015

American community survey. Strong evidence exists that California municipalities are not conducting reasonable voter registration list maintenance as mandated under the NVRA....The letter also serves as statutory notice the Election Integrity Project California, Inc. a registered nonprofit corporation in California will bring a lawsuit against you and, if appropriate against the counties named in this letter, if you do not take specific actions to correct these violations of section 8 within 90 days." The letter goes on to make claim of the following: "Eleven California counties have more total registered voters than citizens of legal voting age population. Based on the review of EAC EAVS report the 2011–2015 US Census Bureau's total American Community Survey, and the most recent California total active and total inactive voter registration records shows there were more total registered voters than there were adults over the age of 18 living in each of the following eleven (11) counties: Imperial (102%) Lassen (102%), Los Angeles (112%), Monterey (104%), San Diego (138%), San Francisco (114%), San Mateo (111%), Santa Cruz (109%), Solano (111%), Stanislaus (102%) and Yolo (110%)."

The situation in these counties is, if anything, much worse than these figures because the number for Los Angeles County up until 2015 was 112 percent, but Los Angeles County official confirmed in June of 2017 that the total number of registered voters is a whopping 144 percent. There are millions who are registered to vote who do not exist in terms of the actual total number of resident citizens of voting age, which means millions of votes could actually have been duplicated and voted twice or more for the same candidate in the last November 2016 election. This is a huge national problem and a system that most likely rigged. Trump called it out, and on this subject, his allegations are correct.

Trump has a philosophy of "I will be the one responsible. I will take the lead." He is very quick to take the credit for a decision that he implements. I have also noticed that he often gives credit to others, and he can be very specific in his remarks about who was responsible for getting something accomplished. He is so used to making the major decisions entirely on his own that to delegate these decisions to others may be a challenge for him. I also believe he knows it is not wise to refuse good advice. But if you can't get good advice from those around you, then you will have to make your own decisions. Most presidents don't make their own decisions without extensive input and research from their staff. This is called wise counsel. Proverbs says in 15:22, "Refuse good advice and watch your plans fail: take good counsel and watch them succeed." In this sense, Trump is not afraid to go out in front, but he should proceed with caution because he is new at politics and the treachery it brings.

When I refer to Trump being a "man's man," I mean he is very direct and doesn't stonewall. He gets right after the tough questions. To the best of his ability, he tries to be politically correct, but his personality is not built that way. Frankly, a lot of Americans love this and prefer it that way. He is going to continue to speak his mind in a frank manner that will never change. This direct approach will produce the best outcome for him. People will understand what he is saying and the sincere nature delivered on the message. There are times when we see other politicians speak, and we really wonder if they believe what they are telling us. Some people call this not telling the truth; I call it just being a politician. This is not Trump's problem. Trump is the most transparent president we have had since Teddy Roosevelt.

CHAPTER 3

The Mainstream Media Helping Trump 24/7 Using "Fake News"

CNN WAS CALLED OUT AND named by many conservatives as the "Clinton News Network." This name stuck during the heated campaign between Hillary Rodham Clinton and Donald John Trump. Today CNN has now earned the nickname "Corrupt News Network." This is not a misnomer or an exaggeration. When a news organization abandons the principals of journalism and engages in propaganda with a specific agenda, then it becomes corrupt. CNN is not alone in this corruption: the *Washington Post*, the *New York Times*, the *Los Angeles Times*, the *Seattle Times*, MSNBC, CBS, NBC, ABC, Univision, and Yahoo News are all on the same page as CNN and following the same "Fake news agenda." CNN and the other networks who wish to keep printing fake news are guilty of "journalistic malpractice." The networks have gone way off the reservation with views only going in one direction.

"Fake news" really now has a different definition. Fake news means to give or create an opinion mixed in with unsubstantiated facts to change what really happened. It comes from many years of liberal thought and directed agendas that exist at these news organizations. The political agendas start at the top management levels and are implemented within the ranks of reporters, and that information is what we readers of the "fake news" must now read in the papers or view on television. Keep in mind that those graduates who come out of journalism schools experience only certain views by the professors and are taught by teachers of whom 95 percent are liberal Democrats or socialists. This carry-over into professional journalism is very obvious and actually dangerous. The American public deserves more than one view, and without both views, all history is changed. With fake news, facts don't matter. The narrative is preplanned, and then a source is given without proof. Another example of fake news is when the media will edit or leave out portions of a recorded event, either an audio or a video clip. This has been very common lately within the news services, and especially on the Internet.

There is another component that is hidden from most of us and what I describe as the "dark, dirty secret." Before I reveal the "secret," let me be clear about freedom of speech. Freedom of speech is really that. In America you can say anything you want about a person, place, or thing without fear of prosecution or dire consequences. Of course it goes without saying that death threats, terrorist threats, and hate speech can land you in jail, but for the most part, we Americans get away with a lot when it comes to verbal or written expression. Opinions are not restricted in America like in many other countries, and I for one would never advocate any further government laws or interference in our freedom of speech. But what happens when the freedom of speech is false, causing harm to a reputation? In most cases nothing will happen to the one making the false statements. Slander and liable are legal legitimate ways to cause someone to cease and desist. Many lawsuits move through the court system. The law is only on your side if you can prove the statements made are in fact false.

Opinions are not considered libel or slander. The statements and information disseminated to the public must contain falsehoods and must cause harm to a reputation or business activity in order to hold up to a charge of slander.

The "dark, dirty secret" comes into play when mainstream reporters are paid cash money or monetary rewards for writing defamatory and even false stories about a person, and in this case, to the detriment of Donald Trump. Who would pay for this ongoing deception, and is it illegal? Some of this money is coming from offshore bank accounts. The second part of the question is very easy to answer. It is not illegal to receive money to write a story about anyone. This includes positive stories or negative stories. News reporters have been paid "under the table" for many years from powerful businessmen, politicians. This dirty secret has gone unnoticed by the general public, but the frequency has really picked up over the past ten years. This is really a fraud to the American public and a terrible trend that is confusing and misleading all of us. This is a dangerous practice to distort facts, which also distorts all of human history.

I repeat, it is not a felony crime or a misdemeanor to write a false/fake news story and get paid by someone else who is trying to bring someone down or ruin his or her reputation. No accountability on the part of the author. The journalists all know this, and they know they can get away with it. Ask yourself: if the money is good enough, why not take a small risk? This practice is a small risk for a couple of reasons. First, if someone writes an article or piece that is designed to sway opinion by using misleading facts or just inaccurate information, the consequences are minimal. Chances of slander suit are rare; chances of getting fired are rare; chances of criminal prosecution not in the legal statutes. Second, proving this action or the general public finding out that money was received by a reporter under the table to write a negative or a positive article has a very low risk. Third, in almost all cases where a reporter does an out and out inaccurate "hit piece" on someone, the worst consequence seems to simply be that the news organization or the newspaper will print a retraction. Most of those newspaper retractions are very brief and not self-accusing.

The word collusion has been used quite often by the MSM. MSM is still connecting this word to either the Trump campaign, which someone needs to tell the MSM that the 2016 campaign is officially over—time to move on a report real news events—or they connect the word "collusion" to the Trump presidency. Either way, the real collusion is between the Democrats, the DNC, donors to the Democratic party, and the MSM. It goes so deep that I believe that they have secret or undisclosed meetings with reporters to invent and build a false or fake story with anonymous sources. Almost all these stories coming out of the *New York Times*, the *Washington Post*, CNN, and MSNBC have no verified source. Or there are supposedly emails or memos that can't even be produced yet each of these stories makes the national nightly news or it is "breaking news."

CNN, the leader in the "remove Trump, resist Trump, and slow down Trump" movement has been the most aggressive against the Trump Presidency. The main goal of CNN is to thwart Trump's popularity and his policies. He is a target 24-7, and that target is not going away as far as CNN is concerned. CNN is not really just reporting the news; they have formulated teams of commentators to stick together in the same narrative: hate and resist Trump at all costs. There is no middle ground when it comes down to reporting on Trump. This reporting has to be "all bad" about Trump, and if it's not bad, we must find an angle to make it bad!

We know that CNN is liberal, and they support liberal causes, and this must also come from their beginning. CNN was founded by Ted Turner, a very liberal individual. Ted's real name is Robert Edward Turner III. He was born in Cincinnati, Ohio, on November 19,1938; he is 78 years old. He attended a prestigious boys' school in Cincinnati growing up and later attended an Ivy League school, Brown University. I state that "he attended"; he did not graduate from Brown because he was caught with a female in his dormitory room and expelled before he could graduate. Ted always got along with the ladies and was married three times. His last wife he divorced from was Jane Fonda, the famous actress and activist. They were married for ten years, from 1991 to 2001. Jane was even more famous for her dramatic protests. Jane Fonda in the early 1970s may have been the most liberal person in the United States; she was dramatically opposed to the Vietnam War in Southeast Asia. She actually traveled to Communist North Vietnam and met with their leaders to show her support for ending the war. This raised a lot of eyebrows at the time, and many Americans labeled Jane Fonda an out-and-out Communist. Anyway, back to Ted. Turner did, however, finally receive an honorary degree later in life from Brown University. Apparently, not having graduated from Brown did not hurt his business success one bit. In 1970 Turner formed the Turner Broadcasting Company, and from there things really took off for the Turner empire. In 1978 Ted Turner acquired the Atlanta Braves baseball team, the Atlanta Hawks basketball team, television station WTBS Superstation, MGM/United Artists Pictures, and he just kept going with more companies. He started TCM Turner Classic Movies, TNT, and Cartoon Network. He started CNN in 1979 as the first twenty-four-hour news network—a new concept at the time. CNN now broadcasts in more countries than any other television news service. The Turner empire is really an amazing story of business acquisitions, mergers, and buyouts. Turner did sell CNN to Time Warner in his later years. He has become one of, if not the, largest owners of open lands and cattle ranches in the world and has become a Philanthropist. The biggest headline that Ted Turner was credited for was his $1-billion donation to the United Nations. The United Nations ended up getting the $1 billion, but they got the money over twenty years. Ted Turner did not give an outright donation like most people thought. He instead set up a grantor charitable lead trust, a popular tax strategy for the rich. The way a charitable lead trust works is really called the "Indian giver trust," mainly because the donors get back more in tax savings than you gave away. Turner set up the trust for twenty years to actually give $5 million per year to the United Nations. Based on IRS code section 170, a charitable trust is considered a "completed gift" to the charity, even though it could take years for the specific charity to get their final money. Ted Turner actually pledged $50 million a year to United Nations for twenty years. $50 million per year times twenty years equals $1 billion. Why is this a good deal for Ted? It gives him a $1-billion tax deduction against future taxes or future taxable ordinary income. Also because he donated his Turner company stock and his Time Warner stock that he owned using this as the assets pledged for CLAT. Now, by using the previous controlled stock as the donation contribution, then he pays zero capital gains taxes on the shares that he sells in the future. The reason he gets the pass on paying any capital gain taxes is because he placed the securities in the trust. Once you have placed the stock in the trust, it freezes the capital gains tax. One last thing: with a charitable lead trust, you are only obligated to give away the stated trust amount in yearly income. In the case of Ted's trust, it was a 5 percent contribution of the trust corpus per year that he declared, so he was giving away 5 percent, or $50 million, per year to the United Nations. Meanwhile the trust could be earning perhaps 8 percent per year or more on various investment allocations. That now gives Ted Turner an "Indian giver trust," meaning the billion-dollar trust could be making $30 million per year and growing each year for his benefit, not just the benefit of the CLAT. The end result is that Ted will get the $1 billion back to himself after twenty years, tax free, and the growth of the projected 3 percent or $30 million extra per year could amass to be $1.6 billon back to Ted Turner's personal assets. Not a bad strategy, having received a huge tax deduction and avoided capital gains taxes.

Here are the financial benefits of the grantor charitable lead annuity trust:

1. Ted Turner receives an upfront tax deduction of one billion dollars.
2. The trust corpus, in his case the one billion, gets returned to Ted Turner after twenty years.
3. The trust assets can grow with no tax consequences and even return a larger amount.
4. Client Ted Turner avoids the capital gains tax on appreciated donated stock or stock options.
5. The United Nations does receive the $1 billion; however, it takes twenty years, and the annual giving is set at $50 million per year.

Some people consider grantor charitable lead annuity trusts to be a tax scheme and perhaps even cheating the federal government out of taxes collected. Ted Turner took it one step further. He actually did not make the donation to the United Nations. Instead, he helped set up the separate United Nations Foundation, not the regular United Nations world organization. He did this because he did not want the United States, which funds most of the budget of the United Nations, to escape from their obligations of paying their normal share of the budget. Therefore, he established this special foundation just to receive his huge gift, which, as I explained above, was not much of a gift at all.

Ted Turner is still currently serving on the board of directors of the United Nations Foundation.

In addition to his masterful tax planning, Ted Turner owns one piece of property that is 920 square miles in New Mexico. It is the largest single-owned contiguous piece of land in the United States. Turner gets tax breaks in the form of "conservation easements"; these are add-on income tax deductions if you own land that will used for open spaces and not commercial or residential housing. The wealthy who claim huge philanthropy and announce their charitable intent are often the imposters of charity. Yes, they do donate, but with a catch! Where is Robin Hood when we need him? In the end, CNN or Ted Turner could criticize Donald Trump for his wealth and perhaps his greed to amass wealth, but Ted Turner, the former owner and founder of CNN makes Trump look like a novice when it comes to avoiding paying the federal income taxes and the government. We could almost call Turner a "fake philanthropist," just like CNN is the "fake news network." They do go together. I don't want to give the impression that I dislike Ted Turner for giving some money away. I just want the American people to know how he gave it away, and with many wealthy businessmen or businesswomen, many times there can be a catch!

When you think about dirty tricks in politics, then the Fusion GPS team fits the bill. Fusion GPS is currently a big part of the fake news media because mainly Fusion GPS actually creates the fake news with strategic research. Not only do its people make up stories without basis of fact, they actually research a story that will inflict the most damage to a competitor, business, or government rival. After that, then they disseminate their information to the news outlets. Fusion GPS is a Washington, DC, nongovernmental for-profit firm that conducts investigations and formulates campaigns of information.

Their clients include business individuals but mainly political parties, political candidates, or political groups. Democrats have been their only mainstay so far. The firm was founded in 2009 by three former Wall Street reporters. Their biggest clients have been the DNC, Planned Parenthood, and the Hillary Clinton campaign. The firm specializes in opposition research. In 2012 the DNC hired Fusion GPS to do opposition research on Mitt Romney. Opposition research is a fairly accurate word. In layman's terms, it means to find out the negative factors or dirt on the opposition and get it out in the mainstream news to damage the opposition. Fusion GPS has been caught producing "fake news" at least once with the Christopher Steele dossier. Christopher Steele was a former British MI-6 employee. It is difficult to verify if he was an intelligence officer because MI-6 is not going to verify if he was in fact a spy or if he ever operated in that capacity. If you recall, the Trump hit piece that Fusion GPS produced with Steele was that Trump visited Moscow several years ago and hired Russian prostitutes to give him the "golden shower." A golden shower is described as naked individuals urinating on someone. The bottom line is that GPS Fusion is a "dirty deeds" group that gets paid very well for attempting to attack and destroy the credibility and reputation of the competition. Some people believe that these types of businesses are creating what is wrong with our country today. Pulling scandalous stories out of midair to attack reputations and not really having actual proof or the facts may be actually backfiring on the MSM. People are tired of reports that are fabricated, and when the MSM takes the bait and goes to press and on television with another "Fake News" report.

CNN has gone way "off the reservation" and just will not report the facts or do their homework. From their standpoint, an attempt to make Trump look foolish or inaccurate is a daily goal. But when they leave out the facts and then get caught in the act, that is where the American public sees their stories as fake news. On one example was after a Trump speech to the Boy Scouts of America on July 24, 2017. CNN reported a quote and then a follow-up comment. The quote from Trump was, "Many of the top advisers in the White House were Scouts. Ten members of my Cabinet were scouts. Can you believe that? Ten." The CNN follow up was, "One of them is an Eagle Scout and Attorney General Jeff Sessions, who Trump neither brought along on the trip or mentioned in his speech." CNN gets it wrong again. Along with Jeff Sessions, Rex Tillerson, Rick Perry, and Secretary of the Interior Ryan Zinke were all Eagle Scouts. Of course CNN did not report those facts. In other reporting about the Boy Scout Jamboree, here is an example how CNN always goes to the negative and "Fake News" reporting. Trump said, "Boy, you have a lot of people here," speaking to the Boy Scout Jamboree. "The press will say it's about two hundred people. It looks like around forty-five thousand people. You set a record." So the *Charleston Gazette* newspaper reported over forty thousand participants were actually there at the rally, which is what Trump stated in his speech. CNN, of course, said that Trump exaggerated the crowd size. This kind of reporting where the facts are not clear and the facts are in many cases the opposite from reality will backfire on the media. When should the media actually get into a strategy of pushing a specific agenda that is helpful? The point is, all the MSM stories are reported to focus on how Trump is not a fit president to be the leader of the free world. The MSM agenda is always focused on a story that makes Trump appear dishonest or a story that will promote the narrative to conclude that Trump is wrong in his thinking about a subject. At this point most of the media stories are detractors and depressing to most of us. The same media does not give or offer any hope for the future. Maybe that is the final problem—that the media is depressing America and not creating stories that can help us overcome a complicated world. The result is, we as Americans are experiencing the highest rates of suicides in American history and reaching the highest record rates of drug use in the history of the United States, and the death rates as a result of using drugs are rising to epidemic levels. Constant bombardment of negative news has a lasting effect. That effect is not what we need in America today.

In my next chapter, I speak of Hollywood and the entertainment industry. However, the reason I did not place *Saturday Night Live*, the weekly television program on NBC, in the Hollywood chapter is that it really belongs in the "Fake News" mainstream news category. For some people who watch the show, this is the only news or news related programming they even watch. Most millennials do not keep up with the mainstream news, or any news for that matter, whatsoever. They don't get or read magazines and they don't get newspapers. Having said this, *Saturday Night Live* has spent an inordinate amount of time blasting and lampooning Trump and all his close associates. But now it appears the writers of *Saturday Night Live* are tired and coming to the realization that the overkill on is no longer funny. In fact, for them it is becoming a chore to keep coming up with Trump-bashing jokes and stories. The writers are bored with writing about Trump nonstop. "I don't want this job any longer" was the general feeling among the writers who gathered at the Television Critics Association's summer press tour in Beverly Hills, California, on a panel titled "Has Politics Made Late Night Great Again?" Veteran comics like Jay Leno, Norm McDonald, and even Billy Crystal agree that the constant Trump-bashing has been boring and bad for comedy in general, but it does not slow down the progressives and the ultra-liberals. There is a difference between comedy and total activism, which is what the show *Saturday Night Live* has changed into. Some of the panelists at the Television Critics Association press tour were frontline writers for popular comedy shows. The panelists included Ashley Nicole Black, a writer for *Full Frontal with Samantha Bee*; Christine Nangle, head writer for *The President Show*; Hallie Haglund, writer for *The Daily Show with Trevor Noah*; and Jason Reich, head writer for the *Jim Jeffries Show*. Reich said while speaking on the panel, "It can get really boring to deal with the same person, provoking the same level of disagreement with everything he does. To try to find a way to go after that and make it funny can really be boring. It's all exhausting as much as it is boring." She pointed out that during the Obama administration, the show could go weeks without using a clip of the president. Now, she said, "I was really surprised when I did find one act that didn't mention Trump's name once. Usually it is every clip where we mention Trump's name."

CHAPTER 4

Hollywood: Let Them Eat Cake Because They Are All Fake

GEORGE CLOONEY, JENNIFER LAWRENCE, EMMA Watson, Angelina Jolie, Robert De Niro, and dozens of other actor celebrities are technically "FAKE." They would have to be fake in order to do their jobs. You see, they are playing fake characters in their roles, in essence, playing someone not themselves. This is also called imitation of life! Nothing wrong with that profession, but you still have to call it what it is; acting is pretending. Pretending, as defined in the dictionary, "is doing something that is not real." The word "fake" is also described in the dictionary as "not real." Fake is not real, and pretending is not real; actors share that reality. The question is, are those who pretend for a living not real as persons off-screen, or are they always still acting? I guess we will never know. One thing we do know about the celebrity actors I mentioned above is they all have one thing in common: they hate Donald Trump. All of them have openly and publicly stated their dislike for Trump and engaged in aggressive name-calling toward Donald Trump. They are not just speaking out; they are calling him hateful and over-the-top names such as," scumbag, rabid coyote, racist, bigot, pathological liar," some of them even comparing him to Hitler. Why does Hollywood get it wrong most of the time? These questions do keep popping up. It could be that they do not study the issues in a nonbiased way. Their biggest weakness seems to be jumping to conclusions, and if they do not like the messenger, then they either ignore or disdain the entire message. If someone they liked or respected more were in fact delivering the message, then I believe they would accept the message itself. They also use profanity quite a bit. I suppose they believe that in order to have an impactful message it must be a message that engages in foul language. I have observed quite a few Hollywood celebrities who are often getting "bleeped out" on the talk shows late at night. Some of the shows like HBO will allow them to say anything, and they are permitted to use profanity.

Leave it to Hollywood and the wisdom of the entertainment industry to not only get it wrong with their views that do match the rest of us, but in reality, the American public just no longer gives a hoot about what Hollywood thinks. It is appropriate that the movie *La La Land* hit the big screen this year 2017. Hollywood still did not get the message. They are the ones in la-la land! I don't see this changing anytime soon. One thing is for sure: the more they get involved and try to influence an election, the bigger hole they dig for a Democratic candidate. The Democrats need to wake up and say to Hollywood, "Stop helping us; we don't need your help, endorsements, or support."

The biggest backfire situation of an example by the entertainment industry hurting its own Democratic party and actually helping the Republican party happened in 2011. If you could blame one person for the rise of Trump and the successful US presidential campaign of Donald Trump it may just come down to one man only: his name is Seth Meyers. Remember Seth Meyers, who was a host comedian at the Washington, DC, national correspondents' dinner? It happened on April 2011. Seth Meyers made a joke that was so profound to Donald J. Trump that many believe it became the driving force in Trump's desire to become POTUS. Meyers's joke was: "Donald Trump said that he was running for president as a Republican. Which is surprising, because I thought he was running as a joke." His other joke, not very funny, was, "Donald Trump owns the Miss USA pageant, which is great for Republicans because it will streamline their search for a vice-president."

Donald took that night in Washington, DC, and that particular joke so personally that he said to himself and others close to him, "I will just do it! I will run for president." Trump had something to prove at that point. Trump has proved this: because you did not take me seriously, now you will take me seriously as I am the commander-in-chief of the most powerful country in the world. The Trump victory teaches us that nothing can be more powerful than determination. If one sets one's mind on a goal, then those goals can be reached, no matter how difficult or daunting the climb may be. If Seth Meyers was deceased—he is still alive at forty-three years old and born in Evanston, Illinois, at the time of this publication—he should be rolling over in his grave. Seth's insults of Trump were effective but to the wrong end. Instead of berating Trump to the point of psychological defeat in 2011, he actually energized Trump and inspired his family also. If I were a Trump family member, I would take personally the negative things Meyers said about my father or husband. At that moment the Trumps united and backed Donald 100 percent. It created a strong support group for Trump to push forward. Sometimes that can make all the difference. Those jokes turned out to be a big mistake for Seth, just because Seth Meyers is no fan of Donald Trump. If he had actually helped Trump, he would be thrown out of the entertainment business. In fact, he is in the group of Hollywood elites who believe Trump is not a legitimate POTUS. On his NBC talk show, he makes numerous negative Trump jokes every night, and it is obvious he is still very upset over the 2016 elections.

Who is Seth Meyers? Seth is an accomplished comedian and has also been in television shows as an actor and also appeared in motion pictures. His late-night show gets decent ratings from time to time. Seth would be considered in the Hollywood group, although he lives in New York City, on the East Coast. Seth is pretty liberal overall and a registered Democrat. He voted in the last election for Hillary Clinton, along with his wife. They were photographed at the same time at a Manhattan polling place. On the liberal scale of 1 to 10, he is around an 8.5. Seth is married to Alexi Ashe, a human rights attorney, similar to George Clooney's wife but not as high profile. If your vocation is human rights attorney, then that career is going to place you on the higher side of the liberal spectrum, and I am sure she has little to say about Trump that is positive. They were married in Martha's Vineyard in July

2013. She too is a Democrat, and neither of them hides his or her allegiance. He donated to Obama's 2008 presidential campaign and has been a vocal supporter of Obama and Hillary Clinton. The Hillary loss was most likely a major traumatic event in the lives of the Meyers. Anyway, so now that Trump is president, I guess the joke is on you, Seth!

Fast forward to today's news, and the "Hollywood Hates Trump" group is backing any and all resistance to the Trump administration. Also, Hollywood is vocally helping the Democrats who oppose Trump and making sure they denounce Trump daily. Make no doubt, it is a campaign waged by Hollywood to take down, remove from office, or discredit Trump. Hollywood believes they are the "order in the universe," and Trump has disrupted the "order." In the words of Darth Vader, "There is a strong disruption in the Force." Life, liberty, pursuit of happiness, truth, justice, and the American way are all quotations from Hollywood movies. Yet today's movies and the Hollywood elites have moved dramatically away from old-fashioned flag waving and patriotism. Hollywood used to be the poster boy for support of our troops, our veterans, the president, and respect of the office of the Presidency. Not so today. Hollywood is running a campaign of disrupt, reject, resist, and speak out against conservative views, and they really hate President Trump. "Yes I am angry. Yes, I am outraged. Yes, I have thought an awful lot about blowing up the White House, but I know this won't change anything." Madonna was quoted on national television at a Washington, DC, women's march and rally. The comment speaks to the general attitude accepted as a liberal and slanted trend in Hollywood today.

George Clooney has been a very big critic of Trump. Clooney is a huge star in Hollywood, and he has many fans. Recently he stated why he was moving to Europe—because he is afraid of homegrown terrorism in the United States. I know, you can't make this stuff up, right? Europe is a safer place than the United States? I don't think so. England, Germany, Belgium, and France now have "no-go zones" where you are actually warned with street signs that if you are not Muslim, you should be warned to enter at your own risk. I can't imagine George and his wife Amal Alamuddin would ever visit those "no go zones." Where they chose to live is in stark contrast to the neighborhoods around London. Instead George kept his promise to move to Europe, and in the spirit of providing safety for himself, their twins, and his wife Amal, they have gone over the top. Amal, who is a very powerful and respected international human rights lawyer, knows something about violence, war, and terrorism. Amal was born in Beirut, Lebanon, in 1978 about the time that Beirut may have been the most dangerous city in the world. Her entire family fled the country to escape the war causing massive destruction and death. Her mother is a Sunni Muslim, and her Father is a Druze. Druze is an offshoot of the Shiite sect of Ismaili. It is not known if Amal is a practicing Muslim. It is not known if George has converted to the Muslim faith. Amal does not wear a hijab in public, so chances are slim she is a practicing Muslim. One thing is certain: both Amal and George are activists for the rights of Muslim refugees, and they do not believe in border walls. George has spoken out against Trump's travel ban and the border wall to be constructed along the Mexico border. The true irony here is that they bought a massive home without walls, but the home is surrounded by a giant moat. They chose to seek ultimate safety in their new home. Their recently acquired home lies in the middle of the Thames river in England, about thirty-seven miles from downtown London. It is surrounded by water because it is on a private island. It is an English country estate on 5.5 acres. It has high security and can be accessed by water or helicopter. The cost of the estate is not known. It is 8,949 square feet with ten bedrooms, eight full bathrooms, and two half baths, and it has a gate guarded with cameras and a sensor fence.

Not surprising Clooney's California home, located in Studio City, California, is a gated compound tucked away in a canyon. The main house in Studio City is 7,345 square feet with seven bedrooms and an equal number of bathrooms. The size of the guest house is not known. I believe most Americans see hypocrisy in George Clooney; at the same time he condemns borders and walls to protect the territory of the United States, he himself is surrounded by security walls and his own private island.

Ashley Judd is another "Trump hater" and a pronounced left-wing activist. She was very outspoken as she appeared in person during the women's march located in Washington, DC, the day after the Trump inauguration, January 21, 2017. She was very upset about a Trump campaign remark regarding Hillary Clinton. Trump called Hillary a "nasty woman," referring to her personality and her negative remarks about Trump himself. If you recall, Hillary called Trump Islamophobic, homophobic, and misogynistic and implied he was racist. Ashley Judd used the "nasty woman" remark to refer to herself in alignment and solidarity with Hillary. "I am a nasty woman," Ashley shouted from the podium constructed near the US Capitol building. Her other remarks were far worse. "It remains for me the worst thing that has ever happened to me in my lifetime. Raped as a child—bad. Re-raped by a political system that ordains a clown—really bad." She was also interviewed by the *Huffington Post* wearing a "pussy hat." Judd said that the same family member of who failed to protect her from being sexually assaulted as a child betrayed her again by voting for Trump.

Rob Reiner is a New Yorker like Trump, only Rob was born in the Bronx and not Queens, where Trump was born. Rob was born on March 6, 1947, which makes him seventy years old as of this writing. Both of these men are New Yorkers and also about the same age; they both had successful television shows. You would think that they would think alike and perhaps have the same political opinions. But that is not the case; Rob Reiner is very outspoken against Trump and his policies. Rob comes from a Jewish showbiz family, yet today he says he is not an observant follower of the Jewish faith. His mother and father were born Jewish, but now his father is a proclaimed atheist. Rob got his inspiration for show business from his family. Also that is how he got his first television role on *All in the Family*—from his family connections in show business. Rob's father was Carl Reiner (deceased), the famous comedian, actor, writer, and producer. His mother was also an actress, as was Rob's first wife Penny Marshall, also a television star on *Happy Days, Laverne and Shirley*, and other notable television and motion picture appearances. Penny Marshall is also very accomplished director and producer. The CBS show *All in the*

Family was the most-watched show on television for five seasons, from 1971 to 1976. It goes without saying Rob is very accomplished in the movie and television industry. He went to UCLA film school and, after graduating, began his career as a writer for the *Smothers Brothers Comedy Hour*.

He is the true definition of the Hollywood mogul. He formed Castle Rock entertainment and produced such hits as *When Harry Met Sally*, *Misery*, and *A Few Good Men*. Rob is a Hollywood superstar. In the recent years, Reiner has become a very strong liberal activist. He is the cofounder of the American Foundation for Equal Rights, which took a stand to allow for same-sex marriage in California. In 1998 he chaired the campaign to pass Proposition 10, the California Children and Families Initiative. He endorsed Hillary in the 2008 presidential election and again in 2015 for the 2016 election.

Robert De Niro—Bob, as his friends call him—is a pretty big liberal Democrat. In 1998 he lobbied Congress against impeaching President Bill Clinton. He is an adamant supporter of Barack Obama and the Clintons. He showed up at the Izod center in New Jersey in support of Barack Obama for president on February 4, 2008, just before Super Tuesday. He has been even more a fan of Obama since he received the Medal of Freedom award from President Obama in 2016. De Niro is also a New Yorker like Trump. He was born on August 17, 1943, in Greenwich Village, Manhattan, New York City. He spends most of his time in the Tribeca region of Manhattan, New York. But his primary residence is on a seventy-eight-acre estate in Gardiner, New York. He owns properties on the east side of New York and the west side as well. De Niro's net worth is over two hundred million dollars. De Niro, of course, is famous for the big screen and many huge hits. *The Godfather*, *Raging Bull*, *Taxi Driver*, *Goodfellas*, *The Deer Hunter*, and *Casino* are just a few. He has spent very little time with television. De Niro is not particularly well informed on what is going on with national legislative and government issues, at least not on camera, when he is interviewed. I would describe his comments as pretty brash, and the result has been throwing insults toward

Trump. De Niro did call Trump "so blatantly stupid" on national television and threaten to punch Trump in the face on the ABC morning show, *The View*. He is really a name-caller and has not revealed his views of the Trump presidency other than to call him names. One issue he will not discuss is his religion. Interviewers are not allowed to ask him questions about his religion. He was raised by an atheist mother and his father who left the Catholic church at age twelve. One thing that makes Mr. De Niro unlike most of us Americans is that he has another citizenship. He has an Italian passport and full citizenship, even though he was born in the United States and his parents were not Italian citizens, either.

Hollywood has lined up against Trump, but here is the question. Is Hollywood really keeping the "A-Team" out front to take on Trump? It appears that the top Hollywood stars are less vocal today and not out front. The people who are listed above used to be adamant about criticizing, but they seem to have passed the ball to Trump haters who are not really the "A-listers." I cite several names that are not at the top, are less popular, and do not carry a high fan base. The ones I refer to have not been respected as performers and, in some cases, annoy most of the American public. Kathy Lee Griffin comes to mind. She is really a "train wreck" as a person. She does not come across as having any redeeming qualities. She is not an actress per se. She is not a successful entertainer. She is not a leader or a philanthropist. Kathy Lee did a very desperate move to promote her career. She displayed a mock severed head of the president of the United States. It was not funny, and in case Kathy does not know this, evil groups such as ISIS, Mexican cartels, and just bad people are actually displaying severed heads of human beings.

Chelsea Handler is a comedian and a talk-show host. The only problem for Chelsea is that no one watches her show. She is now on the Bravo cable channel. Chelsea is not all that famous, and her popularity is not high. She is very outspoken regarding and could be classified as a true "Trump hater." Recently Handler made some remarks about Trump on a CNN interview. I am not too sure why an interview with a "D-lister" is news; however, here are her remarks: "Trump is a big bully; he treats people terribly, He's disloyal, he lies constantly...It's recorded lies; he is unstable." Handler went on to thank President Trump, saying, "I have become a better person and more informed. I am learning. I have the Trump family to thank for that."

I believe that Snoop Dog is actually one of the "good guys" and made a mistake when he created a recent video which displayed a violent act against Trump. Snoop Dog produced a graphic video that shows a Trump lookalike being shot in the side of the head. I guess that is "art"—"gangsta art." Snoop Dog has not done as much in his career as in the past because, in part, he has been helping in communities and helping the inner-city black youth. He has established his own football league to get the kids involved in activities away from the gangs. This football youth league has been working with the National Football League's "Heads Up" program, promoting concussion safety and he should be commended for it. Snoop Dog is not a man of many words, and his political opinions are not that well known, to say the least. It may be difficult to find political positions or arguments that Snoop has stated in recent history.

Rosie O'Donnell has been very vocal and has gone on rampages with vulgar language against Trump. She does call him a liar and a Cheetos head. She has pretty harsh words for Trump. But her career is really not very active currently. She has not been sought out by television or the motion picture industry recently to star or perform in any productions. Rosie got the brunt of many Trump comments from several years back and Trump jokes about her appearance and her weight. She has a weird body type, and I am sure she does not appreciate Trump referring to the way she looks. Rosie is most likely insecure, and that may cause her to have a very bad temper and overreaction to negative remarks about her. Roseann O'Donnell is her given name and she was born on March 21,1962, and raised in Commack, Long Island, New York. It is very odd that so many New Yorkers have so much disdain and dislike for Trump. Rosie is a huge advocate of LGBT rights and is an outspoken lesbian. She projects her belief system and really will take offense if someone does not agree with her. On January 31, 2002, she played an openly gay mother on the sitcom *Will and Grace*. At Caroline Kennedy's Comedy Club, Rosie came out and said, "I am a dyke." She has lobbied for gay and lesbian adoptions and appeared on national television, *Prime Time Thursday*, interviewed by Diane Sawyer, who talked to her about Florida's ban on gay adoptions at the time.

If you have seen Bill Maher's HBO show, he is not a very talented performer. He is considered a semi-celebrity, and most of his fans come from more extreme walks of life than most of the mainstream television viewers. He is host of the HBO show *Real Time with Bill Maher* and has built his career on the interview of newsmakers and political figures. Most of the time, his program formats are about negative stories and controversial people. Bill Maher would call himself a comedian, and part of his regular show will have a comedic monologue. Depending on your taste, it would be very debatable if Bill Maher is actually funny. His talk show is really more confrontational than funny. He makes no bones about his dislike for President Trump or Republicans in general and berates Fox News and Sean Hannity. His level of Trump bashing turns many people off, and his ratings have dropped recently. He has been on the air for a long time, and he has not changed his colors on where he stands or which party he supports. When George Bush won the 2002 presidential election, he was quoted as saying, "If we could just get rid of these religious people, we might be able to win an election."

J. K. Rowling, author of all the *Harry Potter* books and screenplays, is not quite a part of Hollywood, because she lives in England, but she is still involved because I believe there are eight *Harry Potter* movies that have hit the big screen. What she also has in common with Hollywood is that she is one of Trump's biggest haters. The acclaimed British novelist can't help herself when it comes to consistently criticizing the US president despite being a foreign-born citizen of another country. Rowling trolls the news of President Trumpon a regular basis to see what kind of things she can judge him on, and in most cases, these are harsh judgments. Because Trump is under the microscope with the biased mainstream media, you can count on her to jump on the frenzy. In July of 2017 Trump attended a special meet and greet at the White House the media covered the event. J. K. Rowling after watching the news media coverage, accused Trump of not shaking the hand of a boy named Monty Weer who suffers from spina bifida. The boy was confined to a wheelchair during the meet and greet. The sneaky media edited the video clip that showed Trump passing the boy by when he shook the hands of others beside him. When the entire video clip was shown, it revealed that Trump had spent extra time with the boy above the others and gave the boy a Secret Service patch. J. K. Rowling had the following quote: "Trump imitated a disabled reporter once, and now he pretends not to see a child in a wheelchair, as though frightened he might catch his condition. My mother used a wheelchair. I witnessed people uncomfortable around her disability, but if they had a shred of decency, they got over it. So, yes, that clip of Trump looking deliberately over a disabled child's head, ignoring his outstretched hand [his hand was not outstretched to shake hands] has touched me on the raw." Rowling went on to say, "That man occupies the most powerful office in the free world and his daily outrages against civilized norms are having a corrosive effect…How stunning and how horrible that Trump cannot bring himself to shake the hand of a small boy who only wanted to touch the President." She tweeted that remark over a weekend in late July. However, a White House complete and unedited video showed the opposite. It clearly shows Trump bending down and greeting his young fan before he approached the podium to address the crowd. The boy's mother was in attendance at the White House and gave the following remarks: "If someone can get a message to JK Rowling: Trump didn't snub my son & Monty wasn't even trying to shake his hand." Ms. Kelly Weer wrote this in a post on Facebook, slamming Rowling's inaccurate description of the video showing her son meeting President Trump. She also stated, "He's three years old and handshaking is not his thing, he was showing off his newly acquired Secret Service patch." Rowing never actually apologized to Donald Trump; instead she apologized to the boy and his family for spreading the false claims. Rowling deleted her tweets after three days of knowing the true facts.

After seven months into the Trump presidency, most of the bigger Hollywood stars have gone silent in taking shots at Trump. However, Chelsea Handler, Kathy Griffin, Rosie O'Donnell, and Bill Maher, not big the stars, keep after and continue to "dog" Trump. I guess no one has informed them that they are not that highly respected in the public view. Most people view them as the "D-listers." They may continue to believe that bashing Trump and his family is helping their careers, but it actually is having the opposite effect. Sometimes the people get it right over the dysfunctional and misinformed celebrities, who most of the time get it all wrong.

CHAPTER 5

Churches: Captured, Converted, and Committed

IF YOU LIKE GOD IN your government, get ready for the "New Rapture," and these church folks don't mind your referring to the GOP as the party of God. GOP can now stand for "God's Official Party." If anyone has ever locked up the church vote and will continue to do so, it will be Donald Trump. He is invincible with the churches now that he has appealed the "Johnson Amendment." I should add that perhaps not all churchgoers will back Trump, especially many Catholics who are so ingrained in their family past beliefs that good Catholics vote for Democrats. The Muslim and Islamic churches throughout the United States are not going to be as fond of Trump for obvious reasons. The Johnson Amendment was designed to make sure that a church organization did not endorse or support a specific candidate for a political office. The amendment also prohibited preaching from the pulpit regarding political views. The law was placed into effect in 1954 when Lyndon Johnson was a US Senator from Texas. Johnson sponsored the bill in Congress and the Senate. The law included county, city, state, and federal elected offices. If a church broke with this rule, then that same church could be investigated, mainly by the state attorney general and the IRS. If it was determined that the Johnson Amendment laws were broken, then tax-exempt status could be revoked. If a pastor, priest, rabbi, minister, or other religious leader aided in these upcoming or current political campaigns, then also tax-exempt status would be at risk to the church. The fact that Trump has changed this law is a huge step for churches to engage directly in the political process.

Historically speaking, churches were active in America and are much older than the US Constitution or the founding fathers. It could be argued that the US Constitution was based on religious values and most definitely on religious freedoms. Back in those days, it was not acceptable to be an atheist or even agnostic. Europeans who immigrated to America believed in witches, warlocks, and the devil. To be anything other than religious would have been risking your life to be burned at the stake or drowned in a well. If you were void of faith, then at best case you would have been "shunned." Shunning was a punishment where a person or entire family was no longer allowed to congregate with others in the community. This could be extremely dangerous back then because of the interdependence on one another for food, medicine, grain for livestock, and so on, which was vital for survival. Sixteen years after the Pilgrims landed at Plymouth rock in Massachusetts, the settlers voted to establish a university. These settlers were still suffering through great hardships, yet they felt compelled to further education in their new world. The university, when it opened, only had nine students and one faculty member. The school was named after and founded by John Harvard, a minister from England. John Harvard donated a library and half of his entire estate to the newly formed university. John Adams, one of the founding fathers of the United States, attended and graduated from Harvard University, where he studied the following curriculum: Latin, modern languages, classical history, political science, and philosophy. After Harvard was established, other universities started popping up along the original thirteen colonies. A little known fact is that all of the current Ivy League schools, with one exception, that exist and currently operate today on the East Coast were founded by either a minister, a pastor, or a priest. The only exception to the Ivy League list of schools is Columbia University, located in New York City. Over half the private universities in the United States today were founded by a religious denomination. Even University of California at Berkeley was founded by a minister.

The impact and the long history of church affiliations cannot be underestimated in the United States. Most of us are familiar with the "Right to Life" movement. Right to Life typically will gather at churches and do their organizing. The evangelical churches have been the main sounding board and organizers of the group. The Right to Life movement has different operating within 501(c)(3) groups. One of the largest groups is actually located in Southern California; it is the Right to Life League of Southern California. This group will then go out into the communities and walk precincts for a particular candidate, or the GOP, or even state or federal legislation that protects the unborn and fights against abortions. This group was an effective way for churches to do an "end run" around the Johnson Amendment. The Right to Life movement has been very well organized and accepts the GOP as the party of their choice.

Here is the new "secret sauce" with what can now be done. If a US taxpayer donates to a political candidate, that donation is *not* tax deductible. If you donate to a church today, that is now aiding or helping a political candidate get elected to office, and if you give that money directly to the church, then the donation is now deductible. Churches now have much more leeway and can endorse a candidate without fear of losing the tax exemption. Regardless of the repeal of the Johnson Amendment, only one church/religious organization out of an estimated 670,000 operating in the United States was audited since 2008. That church maintained its tax-exempt status. The reason churches do not get audited is they are not required to file a tax return or the 990 IRS form that all other tax-exempt organizations are required to file each year. Religious organizations, not churches, fall into a different category, and they must file a 990 form. The only exception is if the tax-exempt organization takes in twenty-five thousand dollars a year or less in donations; then a 990 form is not required.

According to Charitable Navigator (CN), charitable giving was up again around 5.8 percent to $390 billion, an all-time high in the United States. The CN statistics claim that 32 percent or $122 billion went to churches or religious organizations. I submit to you that figure is closer to $150 or $160 billion. Mainly churches "pass the plate," and those are donations of cash not reported. Also keep in mind that the churches who file the 990 form are the numbers that CN is touting. Most churches don't file the 990 form, so no one knows for sure how much money goes to churches. The average church operating in the United States has only seventy-five members. That seventy-five-member church is not bothering to file a IRS 990 Tax form. Most churches with a thousand members or fewer do not file a 990 either. Because the church does not ever have to file a IRS 990 form, one could see the possibilities for potential abuse. All churches, regardless of faith, creed, or denomination, have the same tax-exempt status. The Christian way means regular tithing, and it is essential in your walk with the Lord. Described in the bible it is called a tithe, and tithe means one-tenth in Holy Bible verse. "The first fruits of our labor will also be given. In today's modern language, that would be the gross pretax earnings, not net after-tax earnings. I am not so sure those who wrote the Bible knew how high the taxes would be in 2017. Especially giving your gross earnings while living in California at 13.5 percent state income tax potential on the highest tax bracket. Also, on top of that, federal income tax rates in the highest brackets makes giving that 10 percent of gross income a tough "road to hoe!" Of course the 10 percent tithe is tax deductible off your annual AGI (adjusted gross income) for tax purposes.

Churches have special ways to stretch annual giving to them throughout the entire year, and over and above the regular giving or regular tithes, there are four ways that I personally know of; they are special offerings, outreach ministry accounts, local or worldwide missions, and salary endowments. First I will start with the "special offerings." Just what is a special offering? Unlike the normal weekly Sunday or Saturday offerings during the church service, the church is going to "pass the donation plates." They will be using the normal ushers at the church to pass the plate for a specific passion or cause that the congregation supports. These special offerings can be for causes that need special or emergency help. Examples are the 9/11 terror attacks; Hurricane Katrina relief; Haiti earthquake relief; and refugees in

Africa, South America, the Ukraine, and war-torn nations. The special offerings are used for local issues in the community like fires, tornado disasters, fires, and even unexpected deaths of family members. Typically, the church pastor will introduce a spokesperson who represents the group or is close to those who need the aid and to those who have suffered. Then this guest speaker will tell his or her story about the events and the devastation left behind in the aftermath. Finally, the guest speaker will make a plea for funds for the victims. Sometimes they ask for food or clothing donations, but not too often. As the people of the congregation pony up the extra giving, a dark secret emerges. The money collected for the special offering does not have to go to cause that was described in church. In most cases the sponsor church will keep half of the funds collected for its own bank account. In some other cases, I have heard from church employees that only one-quarter of the funds donated during the special offering will go to the guest speaker and his or her cause. The remainder will simply stay in the church's main account. Taking the money under those circumstances and using that mathematical formula just described is pretty commonplace and not the exception. The second way a church can increase its giving is though special outreach ministry accounts. This is also a bit sneaky. In order to pull this off, a church has to have an arrangement with its financial institution to set up multiple accounts as DBAs or doing business as accounts. These DBAs are still going to remain under one tax ID number and the same church, but this allows the givers to make checks out direct to the name of the ministry. For example, many churchgoers will give a normal weekly check to the name of the church, such as, "Calvary Christian" (I use Calvary Christian only as a fictional name of the church in this example). Then Calvary Christian Church also has multiple active outreach programs that may be named "Homeless No More," "Beautiful Children," "Elderly Assist," "My Sister's Place Home for Abused Women," and so on, so the people of the church can make out a check to one of these specific ministries. Of course the donors will be thinking that 100 percent of their money gets to each of the causes that they write the check out for. Sadly, and similar to my first example above where I explained how the "special offering" works, that will also not be the case. The people writing checks or wiring funds to the outreach ministries will actually have only a portion of their funds dedicated to those charitable outreach programs sponsored and operated by the church. The church can justify this deception as not real deception. Their rational will be, "Well if we did not have these separate names designated for each passion and outreach area, then those donations would not take place." The third technique a church can use to stretch and increase the regular giving is the "travel business." This is not really travel business, but rather the church will organize local and overseas trips where travel is involved. The church will engage in making arrangement for airlines, hotels, ground transportation, meals, and so on. This is also known as the church-sponsored "mission trip." These can be extensive; two- to three-week trips to the Holy Land, Africa, Russia, Ukraine, India, South America, and poor regions of the United States and Mexico are common mission trips. The money-making opportunities in this venture are pretty obvious. The church makes all the travel arrangements for those going on the mission and then compiles that overall price, which is marked up, to the participants. The church will take in the money difference of what the trip actually costs. What they will make the mission folks pay depends. Normally the mark-up is around a quarter to a third of the entire amount. For example, the actual cost of a trip to visit India may be two thousand dollars altogether. Keep in mind that church participants going on a similar trip to the same places as the mission trip may actually pay the same if they went through a travel agency's comprehensive package as a tourist. However, the church group has a very significant purpose, meaning, passion, and sense of accomplishment.

The fourth way to expand the church budget is through salary endowments. This is a largely unknown secret about churches' inner workings regarding their budget. Yet it is legal and practiced under certain circumstances. The transaction includes three parties: the church, a donor, and a salary recipient. The donor wishes to have his or her son or daughter become a youth pastor or a mission director at the church that the family members attend. This would require that the church has a position open and feels like the youth has the desire, the personality, and the steadfast beliefs of the church at all times. This would also be a job that perhaps many other young people would love to have, but either the church can't afford to pay for the position salary, because the annual won't allow it, or the church is not large enough in terms of members to support the position. Either way, if the youth really wants the job, then usually an older family member like a mother or father or perhaps a rich uncle, aunt, grandfather, or grandmother will approach the church and see if the church could put the young person on a full- or part-time salary. This where it gets interesting. If the church leaders are now speaking with a wealthy church member—and they will know a lot about the person's annual income based on their monthly tithing—then the church would propose the following: "We could hire Billy or Suzy on a full-time basis and pay them around two thousand five hundred dollars per month if you could make a donation to the Church. How long do you expect would Billy or Suzy be working in this capacity with us?" It now doesn't matter what the answer is. Whether they work for one year or multiple years, the church will ask for and expect a donation larger than the cost of the annual salary. For example, $2,500 for one year will cost the church $30,000 a year. If that is the time frame requested, then the church will most likely ask for an initial donation of forty to fifty thousand dollars for each year that the youth works there. They always like a cushion. It is really a win-win because the wealthy donor gets a tax deduction and his or her own child gets a paid job position. That charitable tax deduction can now be carried forward up to fifteen years against AGI, and the salary endowment simply appears as a charitable donation to the church. Nothing in writing can be on record, and if the IRS were to find out that an outright condition was placed on the charitable donation to the church for the benefit of the family member, that would be an example of self-dealing, and the donation would be disallowed. The disallowed tax deduction would be a financial nightmare with penalties and interest charged on a compound basis for each taxable year the donations were taken as a deduction. In the end it is legal for a church to receive the donations, and the self-dealing connection with the annual or a one-time donation would be difficult for the IRS to prove in an audit that it was solely used to pay for the salary of the family member.

Hopefully the examples given above give you some insight into the vast advantages the churches, with their tax-exempt status, are a powerful force to reckon with, and they can be very effective if they throw their support to a candidate for public office in a positive fashion.

Some pastors continue to fear the "pulpit police" or the IRS as a censorship threat, but it is not going to happen with the IRS. It will now be the opposite. Churches will able to exercise their responsibility to speak to those who have the power over us, politicians for example, to articulate God's view on important issues. A very successful tax attorney, an LLM with a masters degree in tax law, once told me, "The IRS is more afraid of churches than churches are of the IRS." The church should not be told that politics are none of its business. One thing has always amazed me—that churches are not being recognized by the business and governmental establishments as a place to learn. Churches do teach just like schools teach. Churches are considered in their own charitable by-laws as "the place of worship," but they are also a place to get knowledge about living life that helps actually society and all mankind. For instance: love your neighbor, give to the poor, aid and comfort those who are sick, help the needy, and do not engage in violence (turn the other cheek). Pastor Jim Barlow, Skyline Church of La Mesa, California, was quoted as saying, "The pulpits of America can save America from disaster." Garlow says his goal is not to use his two-thousand-member church as a political machine to sway elections, but he believes that revealing the issues of the day are important for his congregation and a vital part of his role as a pastor. He is correct to teach and inform because the higher learning institutions in America are teaching our youth to be anti-American, burn our flag, and ignore or resist American patriotism. The colleges and universities are moving our youth in a very dangerous direction if they keep it up.

The Johnson Amendment was never meant to take aim at churches specifically or to hurt them, and Johnson never intended that outcome. Like a lot of congressional legislation, the amendment backfired. The reason religious organizations were affected was because they shared the same tax-exempt status that other organizations shared. Johnson was targeting those other organizations, which he disliked and wished to punish. Congress now in 2017 has a bill to completely overturn the amendment called the 'Free Speech Fairness Act' and it does lift the political speech restrictions completely for pastors. Trump has paved the way, and churches' tax-exempt status is not going to be in danger going forward.

In 2016 there were estimates that around 360,000 churches are active in the United States, with 600,000 total religious organizations and outreach groups tied to religion. Surprisingly, The Salvation Army is basically a giant church with ordained ministers as their regional directors. Six hundred thousand tax-exempts have filed in connection with religion. The big number is sixty-two million worshipers. Need I say more? If a POTUS could dominate the church vote, then that candidate would be a "shoe-in" winner for every election in the future. Another situation that has occurred, at least over the last twenty-five years, is the rise of the "megachurch." Some that stand out are the "Church of Joy" in Phoenix, Arizona; Saddleback Church in El Toro, California; Mariners Christian Church in Newport Beach, California; and Second Baptist Church in Houston, Texas. All of these churches are actually a campus, with multiple buildings, schools, bookstores, cafés, worship centers, children's centers, seniors' centers, and sports and activity centers all located inside the church campus. The Church of Joy has the largest property, with a lineal mile of campus. That campus includes three schools, elementary and junior-high level and high school. The Second Baptist Church in Houston includes a full high school with football fields, baseball fields, and so on. The Catholic church has owned high-school campuses for years, but the rise of the evangelical church has been more recent. If you ever saw the television show *Extreme Home Makeover*, that is what has happened. Huge money donations are pouring into churches. So why does Trump care so much about churches? Simple—that is where the money is, and that is where the votes are. Trump will get more votes and, now that the Johnson Amendment is repealed, newly donated monies can and will go toward political agendas and political support.

Trump won both the white Evangelical vote and the Catholic vote. This vote actually eluded Mitt Romney when he ran for POTUS. Mitt is a Mormon, which is not a religion looked upon favorably by either the Catholics or the Evangelicals. Trump like most of us are influenced by the faith of our parents. Trump's heritage is Protestant and European. His father came from the Lutheran faith from his grandparents in Germany. It is unknown how religious his father's family was, but Trump's father attended church faithfully throughout his entire life. Trump's mother came from a highly religious area of Scotland, where a branch of Presbyterianism, called the "Wee Frees," was her church. This is the nickname of the "small free Church of Scotland" and is still strong today. Now, the Wee Frees had a bit of a shakeup from the regular Presbyterian church founded in England. The Presbyterian religion was created out of the Church of the Covenant. This church and its ministers developed a covenant with the king of England. This was a three-way covenant of God, country, and the king of England. Before this covenant there were Catholic churches and the Anglican churches, now also known as the Episcopal, church. Neither the Catholics nor the Episcopalians ever made a covenant with the king of England. The Presbyterians did make the covenant.

Maryanne Macleod, Trump's mother, immigrated to the United States as a strict Presbyterian. She made sure all her children were raised Presbyterian. Donald Trump identifies himself as a mainline Protestant. Fred Trump was all business most of the time, so he wanted to show his children and his wife that religion was important, but Fred dropped his Lutheran faith in favor of the Presbyterian church due to his wife's wishes. Their first family church was the First Presbyterian Church in Jamaica Queens, New York. This was a big, historic church. It was on the edge of change in the area of just the affluent neighborhoods, so it also had some black members. When the Trumps discovered the reputation of Norman Vincent Peale, the famous author of the book *The Power of Positive Thinking*, they wanted to transfer their church membership to the Marble Collegiate Church where Pastor Peale was preaching. Peale also attracted the New York business community and the New York CEOs. Donald, when he was twenty-eight years old, convinced the members of the Trump home to drive thirteen miles to the Marble Collegiate Church. Fred never actually transferred his membership, but it did become the new family church from then on. The Trump family not only attended regularly but also used the church for baptisms, marriages, and funerals. The relationship between Donald Trump and the new pastor, Norman Vincent Peale, developed into a friendship. Although they were a half-century apart in age, Peale really like Donald Trump. Even now, almost twenty-five years after Peale's death, Trump can't stop praising him. If we fast forward to today, we clearly have reached a point where moral character no longer matters the way it once did. Trump was given a pass on many things that evangelicals despise and preach against in church, such as divorce, worldliness, love of money, lack of church attendance, and profanity. Wait, does Trump use profanity? No, but he was caught using profanity before the election, when the leaked NBC tape emerged with his conversation with Billy Bush where Trump talks salaciously about violating women. The reverend Franklin Graham, the son of Reverend Billy Graham, said it best: "A vote for Hillary Clinton would have been a vote against the church. Hillary Clinton and her followers live in a non-Christian world, and her pro-abortion stance and the effect she would have on the Supreme Court are more important than Trump's moral lapses and would have a devastating effect on religious organizations."

Trump will stick with the Christians and build his base, and if he does not help or support their cause, then he will lose the next election. The good news for Trump is that he does not really have to do too much to keep Christians in his corner. At this point the Democrats are so anti-Christian values that it would be very difficult for any Christian to vote for a liberal Democrat. The Democrats will continue to back later-term abortions, transsexual and transgender rights, and even giving those serving in the military expensive hormone therapy to support their sex-change operations. Christians do not like organizations that call the police "pigs in a blanket, fry them like bacon." The Democrats will continue to overplay the race card and try to make white people feel guilty for being white. All of this does not sit well with the Christians, and they will fight hard to get Trump reelected.

CHAPTER 6

Camelot in the White House— Trump Family

AMERICA HAS NEVER HAD A royal family. Americans rejected the British monarchs when we founded the United States of America in 1776, 241 years ago. But the Trump family and their current presence and influence in the White House may be perhaps reinventing the "Kingdom of the United States." Could a monarch finally be here with the Trump family? King Donald Trump, Queen Melania, the Princess Ivanka, and the rest of the Trump family lineage has created a stir. I know this may be an incredible exaggeration on my part to assume or even mention actual royalty and especially something like Camelot. Camelot had Merlin the wizard, King Arthur, Sir Lancelot, Queen Guinevere, the Knights of the Round Table—wasn't that all fiction? The Trump family is not fiction, and if life was a movie, last time I checked, being smart, rich, educated, and beautiful is probably the group who would be starring in a modern Camelot movie. The Trump extended family and the in-laws appear to be cast in that role. Donald could be King Arthur; Melania could be Queen Guinevere; Jared Kushner could be Sir Lancelot; Ivanka Trump could be Caelia, the future queen; Donald Trump Jr. could be Sir Percival; Eric Trump could be Sir Amr, actual son of King Arthur…well, I could go on, but you all get the picture. Of course "The Donald" would have his Knights of the Round Table, which he has now in the west wing of the White House.

Back to present day, the Trump women are all basically Amazon goddesses, and when they walked out on the campaign stage each time, everyone noticed. Some would say it was a bit jaw-dropping. The Democrat rivals tried to downplay the presence of the Trump family, but there was no hiding how they looked on the live stage. The voters noticed right way, and that was what counted in the end. Time and again the Trump family made a lasting impression. The mainstream media also would not talk about it much, and most of us could tell the media would downplay Trump's impressive family. The facts be told, in the case of all four women in the Trump family, every one of them has had a modeling career. Three of them have had television careers, and one of them appeared in a major motion picture before she was married to a Trump. Melania, Ivanka, Vanessa, and Lara all were successful models. The modeling runway loves tall women, and in the case of height, the Trump family absolutely dominates this one. Donald is six feet two inches, wife Melania is five feet eleven inches, son Eric Trump is six feet five inches, son Donald Jr. is six feet one inch, daughter Ivanka is five feet eleven inches, son-in-law Jared Kushner is six feet three inches, daughter-in-law Vanessa is six feet tall, Lara Trump is five feet eleven inches tall, Tiffany (daughter from Donald Trump's second marriage to Marla Maples) is five feet eight inches tall, and son Barron Trump from Donald's third marriage is already five feet ten inches at age eleven. Barron may be the tallest of all the Trumps when he is fully grown. Why does it matter that the Trump family is tall? It is psychological, really. It gives the Trump family a uniform look of dominance. The uniform look is a sign of strength and lineage. When Donald Trump paraded the entire Trump family out on stage several times during his campaign, it was clever and effective. It showed the competition: you cannot match me! Because of this advantage, the entire Trump family would get attacked for every little thing over and over by the media; joining in on the attacks were Hollywood elites, college professors, liberal "nut jobs," and the Democrats in general. Maybe these groups do not like tall, good-looking people. Is it because the whole left is jealous? Could it be that petty? In a normal world, and based on the core standards that most Americans would expect of a first family of the United States, you could not pick a better group of individuals than the immediate family members named "Trump" or married to a Trump. In contrast, look at past US presidents' family members. In some cases, it is like the *Rocky Horror Picture Show*. I will pick on the last three Democratic presidents. First there is President Jimmy Carter's brother, Billy Carter. Billy was basically hidden from his visits to the White House, and the media made him out to be a lowly educated "hayseed." It was almost a cover-up by the Carters. Billy Carter once urinated in front of reporters while waiting for a plane flight. Billy Carter was a big drinker and endorsed two alcohol-related companies, Peanut Lolita Liqueur and Billy Beer brewed by the Falls City Brewing company. There was strong evidence that Billy Carter received two million dollars from the Libyan government, called influence peddling. Billy Carter registered as a foreign agent so he could do business overseas. Anyway, the whole situation caused major embarrassment to Jimmy Carter because a US Senate subcommittee was called to investigate Billy Carter. The investigation was labeled "Billy Gate" by the press. Second, there is Bill Clinton and his younger brother, Roger Clinton. Roger Clinton is the half-brother of Bill Clinton. Roger was born on July 25, 1956, in Hot Springs, Arkansas. He is several years younger than brother Bill. Roger was an embarrassment to Bill and Hillary early on. Roger was arrested in the mid-1980s for selling cocaine, was convicted, and spent one year in prison. Today Roger no longer has a felony criminal record because on January 20, 2001, the day Bill Clinton left office, Roger was pardoned by his half-brother in his last official business. Just a few months later, in August 2001and just a few months after Bill Clinton left office, in Hermosa Beach, California, Roger was arrested and convicted of reckless driving. The original charge was driving under the influence, but the charge was reduced in a plea deal. Brother William Jefferson Clinton, several years back in 2009, bought Roger a house in Los Angeles. Roger got in trouble with the law again and had his last arrest in Los Angeles County, Redondo Beach, California, on June 6, 2016. This time Roger was arrested for drunk driving and disorderly conduct. It was interesting that during the height of the presidential campaign against Donald Trump in July 2016, no media coverage was given to the arrest of Hillary Clinton's brother-in-law in July of 2016. Could you have imagined what the television or media coverage would have been if a Trump family member or in-law was arrested? Last but not least, we look at Barack Obama's siblings. Malik Obama is the half-brother of Barack Obama and was born on March 1958 in Nairobi, Kenya. He has been very critical of his own brother and said he would have voted for Donald Trump. He was photographed wearing a Trump Make America Great Again baseball cap. Malik Obama also took a copy of a birth certificate from the "Coast Province General Hospital' in Mombasa, Kenya. The birth certificate has a date of August 4, 1961, and the name of both parents, Stanley Ann Obama and Barack Hussein Obama senior. This is very strange behavior from your own half-brother and not a good support group for Barack Obama. In contrast to the past three Democratic presidents, the Trump family appearing like Camelot with a strong support group is very powerful and impressive. The immediate Bush family was not only close as a unit but highly successful, with both George H. W. Bush and George W. serving as POTUS and Jeb Bush as past governor of Florida. However, nothing takes the cake like the Trump family in overall talent—but even more important, it is very apparent that the Trumps always stick together. Using the name "Camelot" on behalf of the Trump family maybe over the top. But this family is over the top, and they are "all in for Trump" and supporting Donald Trump every step of the way. Below is a list of the Trump members who dwell in modern day Camelot.

Ivanka Trump is the daughter of President Donald Trump. By all accounts she is a very impressive young woman. I think that of all the Trump family members, she became the one to stand out the most with the media and press right away. The vastly outnumbered conservative press praised her right off the bat as smart, pretty, talented, and a loyal daughter to her father. However, instead of this image of Ivanka going forward, she turned out to be the number-one target for the main stream media to attack her on a regular basis. If any journalist can give good reason to attack her as a person or somehow imply that she is a detriment to the Trump presidency, you would be certified insane. The facts are so stacked in her favor, it isn't even a debate. Ivanka Marie Trump was born on October 30, 1981, in New York City. She is married to Jarred Kushner, a very successful businessman, real-estate developer, and now an adviser to President Trump. They have three very attractive children. She has kept her maiden name instead of using the Kushner name. Her mother is Donald Trump's first wife, Ivana Trump, who was a Czech-American model before she married Trump. Ivanka attended two colleges, first Georgetown University in Washington, DC, and after two years she transferred from Georgetown to Wharton Business School at the University of Pennsylvania, the same school her father Donald attended. She speaks three languages, English, French, and Czech. Ivanka is five feet eleven inches tall, and in heels, she is as tall as her father at six feet two inches. Ivanka did some modeling in her early years, starting at fifteen years of age. Modeling was only allowed on the weekends because Ivanka attended two very strict boarding schools, the Chapin School in Manhattan, New York, and then the Choate Rosemary Hall in Wallingford, Connecticut. She was able to obtain work as a model on the cover of *Seventeen*, and she walked the runways for Tommy Hilfiger, Sassoon Jeans, Versace, Marc Bouwer, and Thierry Mugler. She has been on the cover of several magazines, including *Harper's Bazaar, Forbes Life, Golf Magazine, Town & Country*, and *Vogue*. She was a feature on the cover of *Stuff*, and she placed eighty-third on the *Maxim* Hot 100 issue. She starred on the sixth season of the television show *The Apprentice* and then for several seasons on *The Celebrity Apprentice*. She was featured as a guest judge on *Project Runway* and appeared in the show *Gossip Girl*. She is the author of two books, *The Trump Card, Playing to Win in Work and Life* and *Women Who Work: Rewriting the Rules for Success*. In January 2017 Ivanka stepped down from her post at the Trump organization to join her father in the White House as an adviser. She was appointed as official government employee on March 29, 2017. A few more interesting facts about Ivanka: She is an Independent as a registered voter, not a Republican like POTUS Trump; and she is friends with Chelsea Clinton and Georgina Bloomberg, daughter of Michael Bloomberg. Hillary, Bill Clinton, and Michael Bloomberg are not fans of Trump today.

Last but not least, Ivanka is very charitable and involved as a volunteer in numerous causes to support working women. Ivanka has converted to

Orthodox Judaism; she keeps a kosher diet. The three children are all very healthy, attractive, and seem to be on their way as outstanding kids.

So let' do a recap on Ivanka:

1. Smart: Wharton Business School, cum laude, author of two books.
2. Beautiful: *Maxim* magazine's top 100. Successful at modeling career.
3. Spiritual: Practicing Orthodox Jew.
4. Rich: Estimated net worth between her and husband Jared is $750 million.
5. Dedicated to family: Supportive of her half-sister, two brothers, mother, stepmother, and father President Trump.
6. Mother: Three children, Anabell Rose, Joseph Fredrick, and Theodore James.

Melania Trump is the current and third wife of Donald Trump and the first lady of the United States of America. Melania is the only Trump immediate or extended family member who was not born in the United States. Melania was born in Yugoslavia April 26, 1970. The part of Yugoslavia where she was from is now called Slovenia. Her original name is Melanija Knavs, and the town she was born in is Novo Mesto in the southeast part of Slovenia. She is the daughter of Amalija and Victor Knavs. The Knavs lived in a modest apartment in a housing block in Sevnica, Slovenia's Lower Savea Valley. She has an older sister, Ines, and an older half-brother whom she has never met. When Melania was a teenager, the family moved to a two-story house in Servnica, Slovenia. In high school she lived in a high-rise apartment in the city of Lijubijana. Knavs attended the Secondary School of Design and Photography in Lijubijana. She went on to study at the University of Lijubijana for one year before dropping out. Her modeling career was taking off at the time she attended university, and modeling took priority. She speaks five languages and is fluent in all five: English, French, Italian, German, and Serbo-Croatian. She began modeling at the age of five and started doing commercials at age sixteen. She signed with a modeling agency in Milan, Italy, at the age of eighteen. At that time, she changed her last name from Knavs to Knauss. She was named runner-up in the 1992 *Jana Magazine* "Look of the Year" contest, held in Lijubijana, after which time she was offered an international modeling contract. The international contract took her to New York City. She started working in the United States prior to receiving a legal work visa. In 1996 she moved to Zeckendorf Towers on Union Square in Manhattan with a roommate, photographer Matthew Atanian. Melania met Donald Trump at a Times Square nightclub named the Kit Kat Club in September 1998. It was fashion week in New York. Trump had been separated form Marla Maples since May 1997. Donald and Melania dated for several years, and during the courtship Donald moved Melania's immediate family to New York. Her parents still now live in New York for most of the year. The couple gained attention in 1999 on the *Howard Stern Show*. Donald once described their relationship in 2005 and stated, "We literally have never had an argument, forget about the word 'fight'…We are just very compatible. We get along." Melania became engaged to Donald in 2004, and they were married on January 22, 2005.

Their wedding was held at the Episcopal Church of Bethesda-by-the-Sea in Palm Beach, Florida. It was followed by a reception at Trump estate ballroom at Mar-a-Lago. The wedding was attended by numerous celebrities such as Barbara Walters, Simon Cowell, Kelly Ripa, Katie Couric, Matt Lauer, Heidi Klum, Star Jones, P. Diddy, Shaquille O'Neal, Regis Philbin, Conrad Black, Bill and Hillary Clinton, Chelsea Clinton, and Rudy Giuliani (perhaps the only wedding attendee to vote for trump in 2016). Singer Billy Joel played piano and serenaded the crowd. Melania wore a $200,000 dress by John Galliano of the house of Christian Dior. On March 20, 2006 Melania became a mother for the first time. She gave birth their son Barron William Trump. Melania gave Barron his middle name, and Donald suggested his first name. On January 20, 2017, Melania assumed the role of first lady of the United States, only the second foreign-born woman to hold this title (after Louisa Adams, wife of John Quincy Adams, who was born in London, England). She is also the first lady to be a naturalized rather than birthright citizen of the United States and the first to speak English as a second language. She is tied with Michelle Obama and Eleanor Roosevelt as the tallest of the first ladies. Most would agree she may be the most beautiful of all the first ladies, but many argue a tie in the beauty contest between her and Jackie Kennedy. Her Secret Service code name is "Muse." Donald's POTUS code name is "Mogul."

Recap on Melania:

1. Smart: Speaks five languages; attended Lijubijana University in Yugoslavia.
2. Beautiful: Modeling career from the age of five and international model.
3. Rich: Married to Donald Trump; his net worth is $3.4 billion.
4. Spiritual: Complicated from her early days. Religion was depressed in the former Soviet Union–occupied Yugoslavia. Raised secretly Catholic, however, she is now more of a Presbyterian.
5. Dedicated to family: Still close to her parents and sister; also devoted wife to Donald Trump.
6. Mother: Has one son, Barron William Trump.

Jared Kushner is the son-in-law of President Trump and married to Ivanka Trump. Jared currently serves as the senior White House advisor to the Trump administration. Jared Corey Kushner was born on January 10, 1981, in Livingston, New Jersey. He is the son of Seryl and Charles Kushner. Charles Kushner founded the Kushner company, which is a real-estate development and holding company. Charles was actually arrested and convicted on charges of tax evasion, illegal campaign contributions, and witness tampering; he was sentenced to two years in prison. Chris Christie, the current governor of New Jersey, was the US attorney, and he prosecuted Charles Kushner. It has been rumored that Kushner had some influence in Chris Christie being removed from the Trump transition team; also, apparently, anyone who was connected to Christie was also no longer considered to be on the team. Kushner would have reason to hold a grudge against Christie for putting his father in prison for two years. Jared was well educated, graduating from Harvard and also from New York University with a dual JD/MBA degree. At age twenty-five, Kushner bought the *New York Observer*, a weekly New York City newspaper, for $10 million. The newspaper has had its ups and downs but, at this point, is still profitable. Kushner resigned from the paper when he took the White House position in 2017. Jared married Ivanka Trump in a Jewish ceremony on October 25, 2009. There were married at Trump National Golf Club in Bedminster, New Jersey. They were only engaged for three weeks before the wedding. Also a few interesting facts about Jared: Jared is a lifelong registered Democrat, and his grandparents were immigrants and Holocaust survivors from Belarus, former Soviet Union. Shortly after President Trump's inauguration, Jared and Ivanka moved to the nation's capital. They both serve as advisers to the president.

Recap on Jared:

1. Smart: Harvard University, undergraduate; New York University JD degree and MBA.
2. Handsome: Television appearances and photos seem to confirm this.
3. Spiritual: Orthodox Jewish.
4. Rich: Estimated net worth at $750 million.
5. Dedicated to family: Senior adviser to father-in law and supporter of Trump family and his own family.
6. Father: has three children.

Donald Trump Jr. is the oldest son of Donald Trump and of Donald's first wife, Ivana Marie Trump. He has two younger siblings, sister Ivanka and brother Eric. He has two half-siblings, sister Tiffany from Trump's second wife, Marla Maples, and Barron from Trump's current marriage to Melania Trump. Donald Jr. was born in Manhattan, New York, on December 31, 1977, a New Year's Eve baby. Donald Jr. was sent to a boarding school early on in life, the Hill School, located in Pottstown, Pennsylvania. The boarding school is a top-notch university-preparatory school and was followed by the

University of Pennsylvania's Wharton School, where he earned a bachelor of science degree in economics. The Wharton School is world famous for having a top-notch business school that rivals Harvard and Stanford Universities in academic excellence. Donald Jr. did not take to the business world right after graduation. He instead moved to Aspen, Colorado, where he hunted, fished, skied, lived in a truck, and worked as a bartender. He stayed in Aspen for one year before he returned to New York and joined the Trump organization. Donald worked on the development of major real-estate projects throughout the city of New York. Donald Jr. met Vanessa Haydon in New York City at a fashion show in 2003 and married her on November 12, 2005. He proposed to Vanessa with a free engagement ring. Donald Jr. struck a deal with the Bailey, Banks & Biddle jewelry store in New York. The store gave him the ring if he agreed to do some promotions for the company. The engagement ring is impressive—it is worth $100,000 with a four-carat emerald-cut diamond ring flanked by two trapezoid diamonds, set in a platinum mounting that has an additional fifty-six diamonds. Donald and Vanessa were actually married at Trump's country club in Palm beach Florida, Mara-a-Lago, also saving Donald Jr. thousands of dollars because they had 370 guests. They now have five children and live in Manhattan. Donald is the executive director of the Trump Organization and a fourth-generation businessman. His great-grandmother was the founder of the Trump company, Elizabeth Trump, followed by Fred Trump, his grandfather, and then Donald and his brother Eric have all been involved. Donald learned the Czech language from his grandmother and mother, Ivana Trump, who was from Czechoslovakia.

Recap on Donald Jr.:

1. Smart: Graduate of the Wharton School of Business; he also runs the Trump organization with his brother Eric; speaks three languages.
2. Handsome: Donald has been on the cover of numerous magazines and was on Television for seven years.
3. Rich: Net Worth is $150 million but is named in his father's will and trust, which has an overall worth of $3.5 billion.

4. Spiritual: Raised in the Presbyterian Christian faith; goes to church on a regular basis.
5. Dedicated to family: Donald Jr. and Vanessa have five children, Kai Madison, Donald John III, Tristin Milos, Spencer Fredrick, and Chloe Sofia.

Eric Fredrick Trump, son of Donald and Ivanna Trump, is the third oldest of the Trump children. Eric was born on January 6, 1984; he is aged thirty-three. Born in Manhattan, New York, he attended the Trinity School his early years. He later attended the Hill School like his brother Donald, but not at the same time; they are seven years apart. When his parents divorced in 1991, he was seven years old. Eric would spend his summers in the Czech countryside near Zlin with his maternal grandparents. His grandmother was Maria Zeinicek and his grandfather was Milos Zeinicek. His grandfather taught Eric how to hunt and fish. In 2002 he graduated from the Hill School. He was actually an active board member of the school after college up until 2013. Eric attended Georgetown University in Washington, DC; he graduated from there in 2006 with honors. He obtained a degree in finance and management. Eric started accompanying his father to job sites from an early age. He learned the development and construction business from the ground up. He mowed lawns, cut rebar, laid tile, hung light fixtures, and did various other jobs at the Trump properties. He is employed by the Trump organization as executive vice-president in charge of acquisition and development. He worked with his sister Ivanka to redesign and renovate Trump National Doral and the Blue Monster course in Miami, Florida. Eric also appeared on the television show *The Apprentice*. On July 4, 2013, Eric became engaged to his longtime girlfriend, Lara Lea Yunaska, who is slightly older than Eric. They married on November 8, 2014, at the Trump-owned Mar-a-Lago club in Palm Beach, Florida.

They are having their first child at the end of summer 2017. In 2007 Eric founded the Eric Trump Foundation, a public charity with the purpose of raising money for terminally ill children. In December Richard C. Shadyca

Jr., the president of the fundraising organization of Saint Jude Children's Research Hospital, claimed that the Eric Trump Foundation efforts had raised $16.3 million for the hospital since that charity's inception ten years ago. Eric Trump was a key advisor, fund raiser, and campaign surrogate during the Trump presidential campaign. Eric Trump and his wife made numerous appearance in numerous states supporting Trump for President.

Recap on Eric:

1. Smart: Graduated from a top college, Georgetown University, with honors. Also running multi-billion-dollar organization.
2. Handsome: Photos and television roles appear to show a good-looking gentleman.
3. Rich: Net worth is estimated to be around $100 million.
4. Spiritual: Eric had a Jewish wedding, but he and Lara also attends the Marble Collegiate Church in Manhattan.
5. Dedicated to family: No children yet; one on the way.

Vanessa Haydon Trump Is the current wife of Donald Trump Jr. and the daughter-in-law to President Donald J. Trump. Vanessa was born on December 18, 1977, in Manhattan, New York. Vanessa was actually introduced to Donald Jr. by Donald Trump Sr. at a fashion show in New York City. Vanessa grew up on the Upper East Side of Manhattan and attended the Dwight School on the Upper West Side, where she was a tennis star. She received her degree in psychology from Marymount Manhattan College in New York City. Her mother was the owner of the Kay modeling agency. Vanessa began modeling at the early age of five and was signed by the famed Wilhemina agency. Vanessa also appeared in numerous beauty pageants, and she was crowned Miss America in 2004. She began her acting career in 2003 and appeared in the romantic comedy *Something's Gotta Give* with Jack Nicholson, Keanu Reeves, and Diane Keaton. She appeared on the TV show *The Apprentice* also. She was an excellent tennis player and is still very good at the sport. It helps her stay in shape. Vanessa also dated Leonardo DiCaprio for a brief period of time. Vanessa and Donald Jr. have been married since November 2005. She met Donald Jr. at a fashion show in 2003; she was then a model and actress. The media buzzed when Donald Trump Sr. went on Larry King's show and actually criticized his son for accepting a free engagement ring from a jewelry store in exchange for announcing his engagement at the store. It made Donald Jr. look a bit like a cheapskate. The couple finally married in November 2005 at the Trump-owned Mar-a-Lago Club in Palm Beach, Florida. Together they have five children. She is also an accomplished businesswoman, having launched a handbag company in 2010, La Poshett, that has been very successful. The handbags are described as "sleek elegance, luxury and grace for both evening and day ensemble." Vanessa's mother and father encouraged her to be involved in charity efforts from a young age. Her philanthropy also includes her brother-in-law Eric Trump's foundation, where she serves on the executive committee. She volunteered on an Operation Smile medical mission in Nicaragua in 2008 along with her husband, Donald Jr.

Recap on Vanessa:

1. Smart: Bachelor of science in psychology from Marymount college of Manhattan. Successful businesswoman.
2. Beautiful: Former Miss America, former model, former movie actress.
3. Rich: Husband's net and her net worth total over $150 million.
4. Spiritual: Also raised Presbyterian and regular churchgoer at the Marble Collegiate church.
5. Dedicated to family: Still close to mother and father; dedicated to husband and children.
6. Mother: She and Donald Jr. have five children.

Lara Lea Yunaska Trump is married to Eric Trump and the daughter-in-law to President Donald Trump. Her maiden name is Lara Yunaska; she was born on October 12, 1982, in New Hanover, North Carolina, and raised at Wrightsville Beach, North Carolina, just east of Wilmington, North Carolina. In 2005 Lara graduated from North Carolina State University with a degree in communications. She also studied at the French Culinary Institute in New York City and graduated with a degree in pastry arts. Lara is also an avid nutrition and fitness buff. She was a former personal trainer and regularly runs full and half marathons for various charities. She is a devotee of the Soul Cycle full-body workout program. She has worked as a journalist as well as associate producer for the CBS show, "Inside Edition." Eric and Lara dated for about six years before Eric proposed in July 2014. Their wedding ceremony took place at Trump's Mar-a-Lago Club in Palm Beach, Florida. Lara and Eric live outside of New York city but have an apartment in Trump Tower, where Eric helps oversee the Trump organization. Lara and Eric Trump were very involved with the Eric Trump Foundation, which was also run by Lara and Eric, but when Donald was elected POTUS, Eric turned the reins over to others; and now they give financial support to St. Jude Children's Research Hospital. They are expecting their first child in the fall of 2017.

Recap on Lara:

1. Smart: Degree in communications and degree in culinary arts; also ex-television producer and journalist.
2. Beautiful: Modeling career most of her life and television appearances, fitness buff, and personal trainer.
3. Rich: Net worth of Lara and Eric Trump is not exact but close to $100 million; like brother Donald Jr., Eric is named in the will of Donald Trump Sr., so again, a very large inheritance is expected—at least one billion dollars.
4. Spiritual: Christian.
5. Dedicated to family: Mother-to-be, expecting in September.

Tiffany Trump is the daughter of Donald Trump's second marriage to Marla Maples. Tiffany was born on October 13, 1993, in Manhattan, New York City. Tiffany was named after the famous store in New York. She ended up living with her mother Marla Maples after Marla and Donald divorced when she was young. Tiffany also attended the University of Pennsylvania and graduated with a degree in sociology and urban studies. She is headed to Georgetown University Law School in Washington, DC, in the fall of 2017. Tiffany has been a model on the runway. She interned at Vogue magazine and has also written and released a song called "Like a Bird." She currently has 748,000 Instagram followers. She is the only Trump relative who has not joined the Trump transition team in the White House; this may be due to her young age—she is only 23 years old.

Recap on Tiffany Trump:

1. Smart: Graduate of Ivy League School (University of Pennsylvania) and headed to Georgetown Law School.
2. Beautiful: Tiffany has modeled much of her life and is now appearing more on camera.
3. Rich: Her net worth is not known, but she is a Trump—most likely a Trump heir.
4. Spiritual: Religion is not known.
5. Dedicated to family: Tiffany is very close to her mother, Marla, and calls her the best friend ever. She is also very close to Donald and Ivanka Trump.

Barron Trump is the youngest son of Donald Trump and the only son of Melania Trump. Barron William Trump was born on March 20, 2006, in Manhattan, New York City. He has grown up living in Trump Tower in Manhattan but attended the prestigious private Columbia Grammar & Preparatory School in New York City. Barron and his mother Melania stayed behind in New York until Barron, age eleven,, could finish up his fifth grade year, but the pair just made their big move to the White House in June 2017. The new room Barron has at the White House may be a step down for him, because living at Trump Tower, Barron had an entire floor all to himself. Barron will be the first boy to live in the white in over fifty years, since JFK Jr. Johnson, Obama, Nixon, Clinton, and Bush all had girls; Gerald Ford had a son, but his son never lived in the White House. George Bush Sr.'s sons never lived in the White House. Barron will attend Saint Andrew's Preparatory School in Potomac, Maryland, this fall. Barron is also fluent in the Slovene language from his Slovenian mother, Melania. Barron was baptized at the Episcopal Church of Bethesda-by-the-Sea in Palm Beach, Florida. Barron is a mystery today and has not been interviewed or exposed by the media. It is a big question: could Barron run for political office one day? I am sure he will be groomed as a businessman and not a doctor, lawyer, scientist, or musician, but you never know what will happen. I suspect that Barron is headed for greatness at some point in his life. He will have many opportunities—far more than the rest of us.

Recap on Barron Trump:

1. Smart: Difficult to assess at this point, but he will be attending some of the finest college prep schools in the United States. He does already speak two languages at this point in his life.
2. Handsome: Photos and public appearances clearly show that Barron is a handsome young man.
3. Rich: Net worth is not known, but being a Trump heir and the other Trump family trusts that have been established would make him very wealthy.
4. Spiritual; He was baptized in the Episcopalian faith.
5. Dedicated to family: Time will tell.

The Trump family and lineage may be prevalent for years to come in American politics. It is conceivable that any number of the Trumps could run for high political office and be elected. If Donald gets elected for a second term, then the Trump name will have more credibility going forward in US politics. New York is a Democratic, blue state, so a Republican like Donald Jr. or Eric Trump may have a difficult time winning a Senate seat. Perhaps instead winning a congressional seat located outside of the five boroughs of New York. Donald, Eric, or Ivanka could run for mayor of New York and perhaps win. I believe the police and fire would support them, along with other union groups. If Donald is successful in his legacy as president, then Ivanka Trump could perhaps break the "glass ceiling" and be the first woman to be POTUS. When this Trump POTUS term in office is over, either four years in office or eight years in office, the Trump children and the in-laws will have had great exposure and experience knowing what it takes to survive and prevail in American politics. This family group is learning more and more each day and, in fact, building a power base for the future. Despite all the detractors and the critics, the Trump family may be here to stay for a long, long time in United States in elected political offices. Don't count out Jared Kushner; he is a registered Democrat and Jewish. Those two things could help him in New York politics. The MSM may continue to "hound" the Trump family and their political ambitions, but it most likely will not work. The media is slipping so far down as a credible source of information that their biased reporting is having the opposite effect. The whole biased media is backfiring on them, and they can't even figure out that Trump is creating diversions for them. In other words, he gets the media to focus on something trivial when he tweets, and the media goes in that direction and spends time on an inconsequential story. While the media is engaged in following the trivia or the gossip or whatever, Trump turns around and passes new legislation right under their noses that they miss or don't report. Trump is playing the media every single day, and he is winning!

CHAPTER 7

Russia, Russia, Russia: False, Fake, Scam?

"Russian to Judgment," "The Witches of the West Wing," "Be Witched and be Watched"…The Russia story is a witch hunt and really more of a plan or a scheme than an authentic story of actual crimes or wrongdoings. One thing seems for certain: it is the story that never will end. The plan of the Trump opposition I mention is pretty obvious after all this time. Who is behind the plan? It is a combination, and it is a collection of teams who are hired and paid to move this story forward. Evidence has revealed that some of the operatives are being paid, and some simply volunteer to keep the Russia story alive. They believe they must keep the story alive until Trump gets removed from office. If that does not work, then they aim to keep Trump from being an effective POTUS. The teams are organized in the attempt to keep Trump from executing his agenda, passing his executive orders, and moving legislation to the forefront with the House and the Senate. Basically, they want to slow him down to a crawl. Yet, we all have to ask at some point: How many Russians have been arrested in connection to the Russia investigation story? Which Russians have been caught, held for questioning, named, or confirmed to have meddled in US elections or colluded with the Trump campaign? Where is the CIA or the FBI in this? Helping us round up these evildoers? Normally the British and Israeli intelligence agencies help us in discovering international spying or hostile intelligence activities against the United States. Neither of those countries' agencies has come forward, and in fact, they have been *totally silent*. Our CIA and FBI work with these different countries every day to exchange intelligence, yet there is nothing from them on Russian involvement, zero! MSM and the Democrats stated over and over, "Seventeen intelligence agencies confirmed that Russia meddled in the US elections" (source: CNN news, March 13, 2017). This happens to now be a false and debunked statement, and questions of why someone put this out to the public have not been answered. It's because most, if not all, of the sources of facts are fake news. The truth is that only three intelligence agencies even investigated the Russian so-called interference. The FBI, CIA, and NSA have investigated according to their own admission. The other agencies were notified that investigations were taking place within these three. The other fourteen agencies did zero investigation into Russia, and they have no jurisdiction based on their primary government function and outreach capabilities in the matter of investigating Russian meddling. Top to bottom can you say, biggest exaggeration to hit the news in most of our lifetimes. The biggest ringleader in the "collusion with Russia" fake news is Adam Schiff on the US House Intelligence Committee. Adam Schiff unfortunately once crossed paths with Trey Gowdy, another US congressman, and it was a decision Schiff ended up regretting. In July 2017 Jared Kushner, White House adviser—Trump's son-in-law—testified behind closed doors with the House Intelligence Committee. When Kushner appeared before the House Intelligence Committee, he repeated his story that during the actual meeting with a Russian lawyer and some others, the real purpose was to lobby Russia about ending the Magnitsky Act and a ban on Russian adoptions. Kushner left the meeting very quickly, within twenty minutes. Trey Gowdy told members of the committee and others that there was no new evidence, and Kushner's testimony provided no new information. California Congressional Democrat Adam Schiff was furious that his personal push to prove a Russian collusion story was coming up empty. Schiff lashed out at Trey Gowdy about his conduct during the closed-door session. Gowdy fired back that Adam Schiff was using Russia as a publicity hound because he was running for the California US Senate race. The facts are that Schiff has done 123 national television interviews totaling more than fourteen hours of airtime. Schiff has been on CNN, MSNB, Fox News, ABC, NBC, CBS, Comedy Central, and HBO. All the media appearances with Schiff have been about Russian collusion. The media has attempted to portray Schiff as a nonpartisan fact finder, but the truth is, he is making up the story as he goes along. He latched on to this Russia story because it helps him build a profile with Democratic voters to run for higher office.

The biggest lie in the whole story, the claim that Vladimir Putin would have preferred to have Donald Trump as POTUS over Hillary Clinton, is just 100 percent false! The motive for Russia or Vladimir Putin to help or aid Donald trump to get elected as POTUS has no basis for logic. The strategy of Russia helping Trump win the 2016 election would be the largest strategic blunder the Russians could ever make since the start of the cold war. All the Russians and Putin had to do is listen to Trump's campaign speeches. His content and substance in all his speeches were the same theme, and all of his promises and goals for the American people would be very bad for Russia.

Let's examine the things Trump said during his campaign as a promise to America and would be a detriment to Russia:

1. A stronger economy, create jobs, reduce regulations
2. A stronger military, increase the military budgets
3. Negotiate tough trade deals
4. America first and not interested in a "world citizen"; tighten foreign aid and direct money within the USA
5. Close the borders, stop drugs and the undesirable people from coming into the United States
6. Energy independence and the United States actually becomes an exporter of energy
7. Proud and patriotic America. Bring back the flag and honor of the United States.
8. Reduce our commitment of support to the United Nations as an organization that has allowed Russia to get away with so many violations and self-centered moves in the past

Look at the bigger picture: when it comes to helping or hurting Russia, Trump's #1, #2, #3, and #6 are killers to Russia. Especially #6. Russia's whole economy is based on oil and natural gas production and sales. If America becomes an exporter—and we are now—of liquefied natural gas and oil, then it is all over for Russia. Their economy is seriously hurt. Bottom line, Trump hurts Russia, and now that the 2016 elections are over all the world will see this is the case. Those who have studied Russian history know that Russians have a fear of occupation and even invasion. The Russians have been invaded over ten times in their history. Contrast that with the United States, except Canadians and British in the war of 1812 tried to take back territory that had been claimed and occupied as US territory.

We remember our history with the invasions of the French Napoleon Bonaparte in the eighteenth, century Poland's invasion of Russia, and Nazi Germany's invasion in the twentieth century. Most of us forget that the Mongolian warlords invaded Russia and occupied the Russians for over two hundred years. The warlords killed millions and made the Russians slaves to the Mongolian masters. Genghis Kahn was the most famous in this campaign. The invasions created the tsars of Russia, who attempted to rally the peasants to be able to fight future invasions with make shift armies. With all those territory inclusions and documented deaths due to the invaders, Russia has good reason to be protective and have outright distrust for other countries. I believe we trust the Russians much more than they trust America. They should have seen and accepted a better side of the United States, considering that we came to fight Nazi Germany during World War II and also came to their aid. Our supplies in the beginning supported their fight against Hitler and the evil Nazi empire. Without our supplies and Britain bringing in food to Russia, many more Russians would have starved. Russia lost an estimated twenty million people to World War II from killings on the battlefront, captured prisoners, and starvation.

On August 8, 2017, a CIA spy gave his account of Russia and the Trump presidency. His name is Daniel Hoffman, and he is a three-time station chief for the CIA. His last assignment was in Moscow, where he spent five years until the end of July 2017, when he and 755 American diplomats and US State Department employees were expelled by Vladimir Putin from the embassy and consulates. Putin had reached the end of his patience after Congress passed more rounds of economic sanctions against Russia. His official cover is now lifted, and he shares some thoughts about the ongoing Russia drama. Hoffman said, "Putin had no choice; given the US sanctions on Russia, he had to show his people he would do something in return. He needed to respond to impose some level of reciprocity on the action the United States took." Hoffman also said that Putin stands to benefit because he can now deploy his counterintelligence people in other directions because he has 755 fewer people to keep tabs on from the US embassies. A lot of those people work directly for the CIA and also assist in gathering intelligence. Hoffman's long experience observing Russian spies at work leads to a somewhat different conclusion about revelations from last year's election. Hoffman commented, "Overall I haven't seen any evidence of anyone actually colluding with the Russians, and I don't see Russian intelligence colluding with a campaign to cause harm to another." He also implied that kind of activity would not be the mission of the Russians or their goals. Instead Hoffman believes the Trump Tower meeting between Trump's son-in law, Jared Kushner, campaign manager Paul Manafort, and the so called Kremlin-connected Russians is somewhat significant mostly for what it reveals about Russia's motives. Hoffman also said, "It pointed to a discoverable influence operation, referring to the actual meeting, rather than some effort to establish a clandestine channel for collusion."

Vladimir Vladimirovich Putin was born on October 7, 1952, in Leningrad, Russia. He is the youngest of three children of Maria Ivanova Putin and Vladimir Spiridonovich Putin. In September 1960, at age eight, he started school at School number 193, Baskov Lane in Leningrad. At the same school, at age twelve, he began to practice judo and sambo, another fighting style. Putin left the Baskov school to study law at the Saint Petersburg State University in 1970 and graduated in 1975. His first job was in 1975, hired by the KGB. When it came to intelligence and counterintelligence, Putin actually may have had the longest training period of anyone in the history of the KGB. His extended training was six years to be exact. His first real assignment was monitoring foreigners working at the consular offices in Leningrad. Putin made a name for himself for his ability to get the job done. He was ordered to report to East Germany and consequently stationed to work with the hotbed of spies in Dresden, East Germany. Putin was in East Germany when the Berlin wall came down on November 9, 1989. Putin had to take charge of burning KGB files before the protestors could get to them. By 1991 Putin had reached the rank of lieutenant colonel, and he resigned in 1991. Colonel is really the highest rank you can obtain and still be a field officer. After the intelligence officers obtain a higher promotion than colonel, they will get assigned to a desk job or a post somewhere like a supervisor. The KGB is different than our CIA or FBI. The KGB officers are considered part of the Soviet military, and they have ranks like the military—lieutenant, captain, major, colonel, and general. The members of the FBI and the CIA and, for that matter, most of the other US intelligence agencies are civilians they are not assigned a rank. They are called special agents for the FBI and intelligence officers or analysts for the CIA. Putin has gone on record saying that he opposed communism; he was quoted as once saying, "Communism is a blind alley, far away from the mainstream of civilization." By March 1994 he was appointed as the first deputy chairman of the government of Saint Petersburg, Russia. In July 1988 Putin was appointed by the president of Russia, Boris Yeltsin, as director of the Federal Security Service (FSB). The ESB replaced the old KGB as the primary intelligence and security organization for the Russian Federation. Contrary to the reports United States by the media and political pundits, Putin never ran the KGB. The KGB had been disbanded by the time he took over as director. Also, what has been exaggerated often about Putin is that he ran the KGB for many years. He only ran the FSB for thirteen months, from July 1998 until August 1999. Putin went on to be elected president of the Russian Federation by a 53 percent vote in 2000. His second term was 2004 and he won the vote by 71 percent. In 2008 Vladimir Putin was now barred from his third term by the Russian Constitution. However, Dimitry Medvedev was elected his successor, but in a shocking move, one day after Medvedev became president,

Putin was appointed prime minister of Russia. This really meant that Putin would not relinquish power. Putin stayed in this position from 2008 to 2011. Then, on September 24, Medvedev officially proposed that Putin be president again in 2012. On March 4, 2012, Putin won the presidential elections again among massive accusations and protests of voter fraud. He won the election with 63 percent of the vote.

Putin runs the country and perhaps will never allow himself to be replaced. In April 2017, Levada Center, a polling organization, found that 45 percent of Russians support the resignation of Russian Prime Minister Dimitry Medvedev. There have been no polls taken on Putin, but his approval ratings are stated to be around 83 percent. Don't count on Putin leaving the power he now holds, and don't count on him leaving office anytime soon. Russians and Americans don't mix politically, and Russia is run much different that the United States. Russia is authoritarian, and the press is censored often. The US-Russia relationship is not good except for business. American businessmen go to Russia all the time. Industries have been started in Russia, and hundreds of American businesses have interests and even numerous employees working in Russia. Vladimir Putin is a smart man and a very capable man, and he is power hungry. The question is, is he more powerful than all our intelligence agencies, and are his intelligence services so much better than ours in the United States that they could actually choose who they wanted for POTUS? Where is any evidence that Putin or the Russians wanted Trump to defeat Hillary Clinton? It just does not make sense. History tells us Hillary and Bill Clinton have met with Putin and the Russians much more often than Trump or Trump administration members. Even as of July 2017, at the G 20 meeting in Germany, POTUS Trump met Putin for the first time ever. It is a fact that John F. Kennedy met with Nikita Krushev in 1961 in East Germany, the communist country at the time. Every president of the United States since Roosevelt has met with a Russian leader.

Send in the clowns: James Clapper, Susan Rice, James Comey, Loretta Lynch, and John Brennan all served under the Obama administration. After twelve months, not one of them has produced any evidence that Trump colluded with the Russians. As civil servants, not one of them has yet shed any light on or cleared up the overall situation with the Russians. What did they do all day in their jobs? If any of these bozos listed above could have stopped the Russians, then why didn't they do something about it? In fact, all of them have furthered a hoax on the public. This hoax has cost the US taxpayers millions of dollars, and now it continues with Robert Muller, ex-FBI director and another official clown. Like Comey, Robert Muller is an attorney and a former federal prosecutor. They have in common that neither was ever a special agent in the FBI. In order to be a special agent, one must go through four months of intensive training at the FBI Academy in Quantico, Virginia. Now this fact, that neither of these two men ever attended Quantico training, does not make them unqualified for the director's position, but this lack of training and knowledge does dampen the trust from the rank and file of the FBI street agents. The initial training from Quantico and the ongoing "in-service" training is a big deal to facilitate proper law enforcement techniques and strategies and keep up with the latest technology advancements. Basic law enforcement is knowing when, how, and where to make the arrest and also having the gut feeling regarding who is guilty and who is innocent, who is a reliable witness and who is not reliable. At this point, the biggest clown of all is Robert Mueller, appointed special counsel. Mueller is on the warpath against Trump, looking for two things, basically. He impaneled a grand jury in Washington, DC, to probe Trump and alleged connections to Russia. Mueller is coming up short on any proof that the Russians could have changed or made a difference in the actual votes going to Trump versus Hillary, so he only has two items left. Item #1: Did Trump collude with Russian intelligence agencies or professional spies connected to Russia that would help him gain an advantage over Hillary Clinton in the general election? This is most likely not going to be a successful avenue for Mueller. It is too difficult to prove this, and he would have to discover the actual names of the spies or Russian intelligence officers, and that is a long shot. I doubt Mueller has access to recorded conversations between Trump and Russians, and if the FBI bugged Trump's phone conversations without probable cause, then people in the FBI or whatever agency did the bugging will be going to jail. Item #2: Mueller is searching for financial ties in the past that may have been part of illegal dealings with the Russians. That could be the case with perhaps a Trump-affiliated company, but I highly doubt it. Trump builds golf resorts, hotels, and residential and commercial office buildings, so far he is not building any of those in Russia. His private operating foundation, "Trump Foundation," was not involved with any countries overseas, because his foundation did not have "worldwide missions status." That means your charity can't support projects outside of the United States, only charitable causes located inside the United States. That investigation of Trump is also a long shot and would go nowhere. Unless something totally comes out of the blue about Trump or is fabricated with lies and half-truths, then the investigation is going to never implicate Trump directly.

Perhaps even more than typical law enforcement actions, regarding federal statutes, is the area of counterintelligence. Counterintelligence is not law enforcement. Counterintelligence is countering the intelligence operations or "spying" from foreign countries taking place in the United States or on US property and military bases abroad. Spies have been around since the beginning of civilization. Roman and Greek spies are referred to in the ancient writings. China talks about spies from the dawn of their civilization, and the Japanese were famous for the silent and deadly assassins, the ninjas. During World War II and even after the war, the OSS, Office of Strategic Services, run by the Department of Defense, mainly directed by the US Army, wanted authority to take over surveillance of German and Japanese spies. "Wild Bill" Donovan was the founder and head of this organization. Mr. Donovan reached the rank of major general in the US Army. Donovan wanted to catch and thwart spies and future spying operations in the United States. The current FBI director would have none of this. J. Edgar Hoover put his foot down with both Presidents Harry Truman and (later) Dwight D. Eisenhower. Hoover prevailed and refused to give up this responsibility to the OSS.

Instead it was determined that the FBI would handle domestic counterintelligence, and the OSS, now called the CIA, would handle intelligence operations in foreign counties. In the end the FBI won out in the battle for jurisdiction, but it created a problem in the minds of intelligence and counter-intelligence officers. The problem lies in the additional layer of legality. This legality makes the US Department of Justice the overseer of counterintelligence activities. The Justice Department monitoring and supervision restricts the secrecy of the activity. Other countries do not have their foreign counter-intelligence service operatives and agents under a department of justice like in the United States. The logic tells us that the more people with "secret" or "top secret clearance" who know the details about a foreign intelligence spying, the greater the potential for leaks.

During the 2016 elections and the so-called Russian interference investigations, Loretta Lynch as attorney general and Crowd Strike, an Irvine, California-based firm, were in charge of forensic computer investigations regarding the hacking of DNC emails. Crowd Strike is described as having the responsibility for monitoring the DNC and, if and when they were attacked by hackers, Crowd Strike would alert the DNC members. An interesting question is, if the Justice Department's Loretta Lynch was involved, why was the FBI not involved? They would have jurisdiction in this case because a crime is being committed if computers are hacked. It would not matter if it were Democratic computers or if it were Republican computers; the FBI would be the best choice to stop the hacking. Crowd Strike becomes very suspect in the whole hacking situation because Crowd Strike has accused the Russians of hacking, yet it has not produced hard evidence of this. Others have claimed to have seen evidence that Crowd Strike is partly responsible for creating the false Russia story.

The DNC e-mails were leaked to the mainstream press involving Hillary Clinton as the favored choice as candidate for POTUS over Bernie Sanders. These were leaked by WikiLeaks and not by any other organization. WikiLeaks has stated several times, as has Julian Assuage, that these captured e-mails were not from Russia or the Russian government. There is more evidence that Seth Rich, the murdered DNC staffer, copied the e-mails and gave them to WikiLeaks. The times of capture of the e-mails are indicated as US Eastern time and not a Russia time zone, just as one piece of evidence. The e-mails revealed that the DNC was unfairly favoring Hillary Clinton to win the nomination for POTUS and that Bernie Sanders did not have a chance of winning. The Bernie Sanders campaign was in the dark and unaware of the plot.

The real Russians are coming! With all the focus on the media story, Special Investigator Robert Muller, the Russians, Putin, and the Trumps, America should really concentrate on what the Russian military is up to. With all this focus on the unimportant and "collusion delusion" Trump-Russia story, why aren't the MSM focusing on reporting on how far Russia is advancing to even attack the United States? Can Russia attack anywhere in the world today, like the United States? Many experts believe we are falling behind and may not understand Russia's military capabilities. On July 19, 2017, Russia's Su-35 fighter jet performed at the MAKS Russia air show, and the results were astounding. The spectators were mystified, and the maneuvers themselves made you want to pick your jaw up off the ground. This fighter jet performed stunts that have never been seen before, and aerodynamic rules seemed to be absolutely broken. The fighter jet appeared suspended in midair and pointed in the opposite direction of where it was heading. It performed high over the town of Zhukovsky, Russia, just outside of Moscow. The Su-35 is known to NATO as the Flanker-E, an updated version of the 1980s-era Su-27 Flanker. The description of the flight and the maneuvers are as follows.

At 1:35 p.m., Russian time, the Su-35 begins what is called a "Cobra Turn" described as where the aircraft performs a pull-up, but instead of returning to level flight, the pilot applies rudder or thrust vectoring and turns downward, leaving a baffling result, especially to those who spend time flying aircraft. Then at the 1:56 mark, the pilot appears to perform a common Russian fighter technique, the "Pugachev's Cobra" maneuver, in which he points the nose of the plane straight up before returning the plane to level flight. It appears to be floating in midair. Then the pilot uses his engines and control surfaces to put the plane into a slow horizontal spin. I did say a horizontal spin and not a vertical spin or dive. Then the pilot does the same spin for the second time. The last and final stunt is the most spectacular move of all. The pilot suddenly jerks the nose of the Su-35 straight up, and then the plane flips around in midair while momentum still carries the plane forward. Then the plane pirouettes into a spiraling dive, but the pilot regains the energy from the dive itself. The Su-35 can accomplish these feats because the two powerful engines together generate 63,800 pounds of thrust at max power. The engines also have the capability to be vectored in two different directions at any given time. This separate vectoring gives it super maneuverability. Based on the MAK air show, the SU-35 has demonstrated superior maneuverability over the Lockheed Martin F-35 fighter used for the US Air force. The United States' F-22 A Raptor is the premier fighter airplane for the future because it is stealth, and also extremely expensive. The SU-35 is not totally stealth.

The Russians are developing space weapons, lasers, and particle beams. These Russian advancements will basically knock the ICBMs and even the short-range missiles out of the sky. The lasers can also be utilized to attack vehicles and troops by burning them up in the field of battle. The tanks and armored vehicles can turn lights mounted on the vehicles. Buried inside the lights themselves are actually laser lights; if someone looks at the light long enough, then the hidden laser can be directed to the eyeballs of the enemy. After five seconds the laser will burn out the retinas of the enemy, blinding them—and they will not regain slight again but will be blind forever. Russia is still very aggressive against the Ukraine. On July 27, 2017, the Russians launched a commercial-sized drone fitted with a grenade made of thermite. It was only a hand grenade. Regardless of the small size of the grenade, the explosion blew up an ammo dump and blew up a uranium depot in the Eastern Ukraine, causing one billion dollars in damage losses to the Ukraine. This was a devastating blow to the country. Amateur video of the incident posted on YouTube shows a raging fire spewing out of control; also, the explosion hit artillery rockets and caused a large shock wave. One person was killed, and five were injured. The drone was believed to have carried a ZMG-1 thermite grenade. Thermite is a combination of iron oxide and aluminum powder; it burns very hot and is perfect for setting off surrounding munitions. The ammo dump is just about sixty miles from the Russian/Ukrainian border at the Balakliya military base. This attack also shows that small drones can cause major damage in future wars.

So now America's Democrats have sanctioned Russia three different times in the last seven months, and Republicans even joined in because the Russians supposedly hacked the US elections on November 8, 2016—or so the media and people in the US government keep announcing. These despicable Russian deeds are being exploited to still blame the Trump administration, even though no one has produced any proof or caught a Russian subject who did the hacking. No arrests, and still in total there is "confusion about the collusion." The result was we pushed the Russian government to counter our sanctions, and they have expelled 755 US government subjects from the entire country of Russia. This now makes the United States virtually blind when it comes to keeping tabs on Russia. I would assume at least one hundred CIA personnel were also expelled, which shuts down our Russia spy network. The State Department personnel who were kicked out of Russia will also hurt our ability to really understand where the Russians are heading politically, militarily, and in the scope of the world picture.

CHAPTER 8

Nicknames Are How Trump Keeps Winning

ONLY DONALD TRUMP CAN CALL people names and give them nicknames that others repeat, or join in on the intended insult, and point out the faults of his adversaries. For everyone else who tries to mimic Trump, it just doesn't work for them. Others have attempted to fight fire with fire, but they can't pull it off. Most of us are amazed how he gets away with it. Donald John Trump had a nickname for several years, "The Donald." Interesting that this name has not been used much lately and has never been used by the MSM since Trump ran for POTUS. Just the use of the name "The Donald" made Trump a different person. Trump never rebuffed the name in public. I don't know if he liked the nickname "The Donald"; perhaps he even gave it to himself. One thing is for sure, though: Donald Trump loves to invent nicknames for others and for all occasions; those nicknames are negative to those individuals. Crooked Hillary, Crying Chuck, Lying Ted, Little Marco, Pocahontas, Low-energy Jeb Bush, "Fake News," Al Gore "the Weatherman"—all of these labels define his attitude, but at the same time they assist Trump every day with his message. The message is: if you are not with me and you are opposed to my agenda, then we have a problem. If we have a problem and you insult, attack, or defame me, then you will suffer my wrath with a negative nickname. This is very effective, in case you have not been watching the television news, social media, radio shows, and broadcasting in general. The use of the nickname and the timing of calling out each one can also be very effective. Megan Kelly, the famous and very successful television Fox News Host (Megan Kelly has left Fox News Channel and currently has her own show on NBC), took on Donald Trump in the name-calling arena. She was a moderator for one of the presidential debates, between candidate Donald Trump and candidate Hillary Clinton. Right off the bat she accused Donald Trump of using names for women in a derogatory manner. She started the first question of the debate to Mr. Trump: "You have referred to women as 'dogs, fat pigs, disgusting animals and slobs.'" At the time, many of us may have thought this exchange alone would have taken Trump down, and he would never really have a chance to beat Hillary ever in the general election. Of course, if we fast forward to today, Hillary lost the election and Megan Kelly has a failing television show that is on the brink of being canceled. The moral of this story, which repeats itself over and over again, is do not try to trade insults with Donald Trump—you will lose every time. Trump says things that others are not willing to say without fear, or Trump will come up with names or comments that are more impactful than the comments of his rivals.

Name-calling goes both ways. Trump was hit by name-calling and negative labels of him immediately by the press liberals and even by his Republican opponents. It took Trump a while to start fighting back. Because Trump is such a strong brawler in this area, he will continue to dominate all these opponents, and he will win his arguments almost every time. Donald will go on the attack with a person, a place, and even over things—he covers it all. He will disagree with crowd sizes, attendance, celebrity statements, whole countries, world leaders, and so on; nothing is out of bounds. Using the nicknames brings shock value that gets Trump though his speeches and when he is questioned. Those people who don't understand the strategy or the tactic of this do not have a true grasp where Trump is taking the conversation. Consequently, I believe Trump has the most negative nicknames said about him of any president in past history. This will continue because certain groups will never accept Trump; they will use their own nicknames as part of the resistance movement and the "dump Trump" movement.

The names that have come from the Internet and Hollywood for "The Donald" are:

1. Cheeto Head
2. Agent Orange
3. Boss Tweet
4. Cheetos-in-Chief
5. Benedict Donald
6. Darth Hater
7. Donald Chump
8. Genghis Can't
9. The Great White Dope
10. Hair Furher
11. The Lone Deranger
12. The Lyin' King
13. President Gold Man Sucks
14. Prima Donald
15. Pudgy McTrump
16. The Talking Yam
17. Tangerine Tornado
18. Tie-Coon
19. Trumplethinskin
20. Trumpty Dumpty
21. Tweeter-in-Chief
22. Fart of the Deal
23. Tweeter Tweeter Pumpkin Eater
24. Putin's Puppy
25. Hair Scare

Dr. Anna Gladkova, PhD, who teaches at the University of New England wrote a 2002 paper on the various nicknames for United States Presidents up until the forty-third president, George Walker Bush. She came up with 430 nicknames; some were negative, and many were positive. There were names like "Tricky

Dick" for Richard Millhouse Nixon, "Slick Willy" and "Bubba" for William Jefferson Clinton, and Honest Abe for Lincoln; so Trump fits in for presidents getting nicknames. It will most interesting if anyone in the media gives him a positive nickname ever during this presidency. I have come up with a few:

1. Get 'er Done Donald
2. The MSM Masher
3. Swamp Drainer
4. Dem Demo Man
5. Trumpintator
6. Master Wall Builder
7. Master Debater
8. King of Zing
9. Mexico's Nightmare
10. ISIS Nightmare
11. Hillary's Nightmare
12. Mr. President
13. The Trump Card

THE INSULT GAME

Many politicians in the past have been the subject of insults and remarks. In many cases the famous recorded remarks and comebacks have come from the most famous leaders. Below are some examples:

1. Lady Astor of England once said to Winston Churchill, "Winston, if you were my husband, I'd put poison in your coffee." Churchill replied, "Nancy, if you were my wife, I'd drink it."
2. Abraham Lincoln was once called two-faced: Lincoln's comeback was, "I leave it to my audience. If I had another face, do you think I would wear this one?"
3. Noel Coward once said to Edna Ferber, "Edna, you look almost like a man." Edna replied, "So do you."

4. Bessie Braddock said to Winston Churchill, "Winston, you are disgusting and drunk!"
    Churchill replied, "I may be drunk, but in the morning I will be sober, and you, madam, will still be ugly."
5. A drunk man once said to Louise Parker, "I can't bear fools." Parker replied, "Apparently your mother could!"
6. Reverend Edward Everett Hale, when asked if he prayed for the senators, said, "No. I look at the senators and pray for the country."
7. A member of the English Parliament asked, "Mr. Churchill, must you always fall asleep while I'm speaking?" Churchill replied, "No, it's purely voluntary."
8. A reporter asked Gandhi, "What do you think of Western civilization?" Gandhi replied, "I think it would be a good idea."
9. Kurt Vonnegut once said to an interviewer, "If your brains were made of dynamite, there wouldn't be enough to blow your hat off."
10. Grouch Marx said, "I never forget a face, but in your case, I'll be glad to make an exception."
11. Mark Twain said, "I didn't attend the funeral, but I sent a nice letter saying I approved of it."
12. A reporter told Babe Ruth that he made more money than President Hoover. Babe Ruth responded, "Maybe so, but I had a better year than he did."

Republicans as a group seem to bring out some of the worst names from Democrats and also the mainstream media. Politicos will tend to dehumanize their opponents, so they will use language that will treat them with less respect than they deserve. Republicans have been called subhuman, mongrels, troglodytes, Neanderthals, scum of the earth, morons, brain-dead, and delusional, to name a few. The goal of all this is to denigrate Republicans as less than human beings. Hillary Clinton used the phrase "basket of deplorables," referring to the people who would follow and vote for Donald Trump. The main stream media has been digging a hole for itself because people know when they are being insulted. Sometimes it almost appears the main stream media does not realize that these people are not ignorant. When it comes down to political and moral issues, the media will come up with a number of ways to falsely describe people who disagree with their views. In other words, the media will demonize those who don't line up with their views. They will imply that their opponents are both evil and stupid at the same time.

CHAPTER 9

Radical Islam, North Korea, Terrorism

RADICAL ISLAM IS NOW MOST definitely connected to terrorism. There is no longer a way to hide this to the public. The word "jihad" means "holy war." It doesn't mean sit down and have tea together or let's do lunch. It means go to war. It is a call to action. This war cry is now waged with a particular group called the infidels, or nonbelievers of Islam. However, the call to action, or jihad, has been expanded. It now includes a resolve that you must not only be a believer to not expect or suffer jihad; you must now believe in the old order of sharia or the laws of sharia. The word "sharia" means the "word of the path." It is based on Islam's holy book, the Quran; the interpretation is called "fikh." The fikh is done through Muslim scholarship and teachings.

Sharia law is more dangerous than terror cells or the jihad in the long run. So how could it be more dangerous than act of terrorism or even out-and-out violent crimes? Because sharia provides a legal standing, and that is why it is called a law. Under terrorism if someone carries it out, you will go to prison for attempting, planning, and completing the task. If you kill others by using terrorism, you can even get the death penalty. Some countries, including the United States, have the death penalty for causing the death of another person. Sharia law has numerous laws that are punishable by death, and it is all legal under the sharia courts. There are numerous acts against Islam and then things that are allowed under Sharia that would be crimes in normal society. Punishments like whippings and cutting off hands are allowed; so are beheadings and stoning—stoning is most likely to be enacted against women. Stoning is mainly implemented if a woman commits adultery. If a man commits adultery, the punishment is not severe. It can be jail time or a shunning by the imam for a period of time. Blasphemy is another offense that can cause a woman to be executed through stoning. A man can be punished for blasphemy, but his execution would be through beheading. There are numerous other ancient practices of sharia that most of us would consider barbaric. Here are some offenses of the laws under sharia: Criticizing the Quran is punishable by death. Criticizing Muhammad or denying he is a prophet is punishable by death. Criticizing or denying Allah is punishable by death. A Muslim who becomes a non-Muslim is punishable by death. A non-Muslim who marries a Muslim woman is punishable by death. A non-Muslim who leads a Muslim away from Islam is punishable by death. A girl's clitoris should be cut. Muslim men have sexual rights to any woman not wearing a hijab. A woman or girl who has been raped cannot testify in court against her rapist. Testimonies of four male witnesses are required to prove rape of a female, A female found guilty of adultery is punishable by death. A man can beat his wife for insubordination. A woman cannot drive a car; it leads to upheaval. A woman cannot speak alone to a man who is not her husband or relative. A man can marry an infant girl and consummate the marriage when she is nine years old. Muslims are required to practice the "Zagat," which is giving alms to the poor but requires giving only to other Muslims and not to others outside of Islam. I will speak more about the Zagat in the church chapter of the book. The list of sharia crimes and offenses goes on, and the list of sharia laws are even longer than expressed or stated in this book.

If these laws and violations don't scare you, they should. What if we had all these laws and active courts that were practicing sharia law in the United States? Don't look too far from our shores because there are now over one hundred active sharia courts in the United Kingdom and growing. Basically sharia law is in the penetration phase. Muslim imams in the United Kingdom now outnumber Christian pastors. The Muslims of Britain started demanding that sharia replace British common law in 2011. Birmingham, South London,

Leeds, Liverpool, Derby, Bradford, Sheffield, Leicester, and other towns all now post signs saying, "You are entering a sharia-controlled zone." England has tolerated these now-segregated communities, and the end result is a disaster. Now one-third of Britain's high-security prison inmates are Muslims. It may be just a matter of time until Britain and other European counties have replaced their common laws with sharia. Check your Greek history and go back to days when Greece was at war with Troy. Troy was located where Turkey is today. Anyway, the Greeks offered a present to the citizens and the king of Troy. It was a giant wooden horse "The Trojan Horse." They rolled the giant horse inside the walls of Troy. Greek soldiers were hiding inside of the horse. While the Trojans were asleep, the Greeks attacked and killed the Trojan soldiers and took control of the capital of Troy. This unfortunately is happening in Britain. The Muslims have been let in, and they intend to take over. The mayor of London is Muslim, and the National Union of Students (NUS) refused to condemn ISIS. A shocking statistic in London, England, is the number of recent acid attacks on common civilians and there use of corrosive substances on the people. Bottles of acid are increasingly used as weapons in the United Kingdom. In 2016 there were 450 attacks, the most ever in recorded history. So far this year, in the first four months, there have been one hundred attacks. In Great Britain most of the attacks have been on men, but it is estimated, because most times the assailant gets away, that these are in fact Muslim men doing the attacks. The global pattern is much different when it comes to the use of acid or corrosives. Globally, and specifically in the Middle East, the pattern is attacking young women and girls who reject males' sexual advances or marriage proposals or have possible disputes over dowry-related issues.

The London attacks are more preplanned or even used in robberies and other violent reprisals. The London mayor, Sadiq Kahn, says he is pushing for tougher sentences for assailants using acid. The London retailers are now considering licensing the purchase of sulfuric acid. However, other caustic substances can be purchased on the open market today that replace sulfuric acid. The final results of acid attacks are horrific as one could imagine. The victim is often disfigured and may have to undergo multiple skin grafts or operations to get back to a normal life.

Welcome to Dearborn, Michigan—sharia has begun in Michigan. Reports of actual Islamic honor killings and botched honor killings are already taking place in Michigan. Honor killing, also spelled honour, is the homicide of a member of a family, due to the fact that the family member brought shame or dishonor upon the family. This is also known as a revenge killing for bringing dishonor to the family. Most of the honor killings—over 90 percent—are against women. This means that the women will be killed or suffer severe punishment. Many members of the family can be involved, and they would have a family council to decide. Here are some of the violations that some women could be guilty of to be the subject of an honor killing: refusing to enter into an arranged marriage, having sex outside marriage, becoming the victim of rape, seeking a divorce (only men can seek divorce), dressing in ways that are inappropriate, having nonheterosexual relations, and renouncing the faith and teachings of Islam. Murder is not always the end punishment; other punishments would include acid attacks, abduction, mutilations, and beatings. The methods of homicide are as follows: stoning, stabbing, beating, burning, beheading, hanging, throat slashing, acid attack, shooting, and strangulation. Hidden among domestic-violence cases reported in America or accidents reported are honor killings. Twenty-seven actual honor killings were reported by the Department of Justice in 2015. Most who investigate these crimes believe that the cover-up of these crimes is widespread. Most of these victims are young women. According to the "Creeping Sharia" website, crimes are being committed in the name of Islam. A February 4, 2017, article on this site reports that Muslim girls have been killed for having non-Muslim boyfriends, and the Dearborn police have covered it up. Police have not attempted to find the family members behind the homicides.

Another brutal reality of radical Islam and the global jihad is that these jihadists have no problem dying in the name of Allah. They are suicide bombers; they will kill themselves gladly in the name of Allah to carry out the jihad. How can you fight terror if they live next door and will kill themselves just so they can kill you? Martyrdom is a part of the Islamic faith, and the opportunity to die in the service and delight of Allah is the ultimate reward. All Muslims are taught that this is the highest honor and receives the highest reward in heaven.

North Korea is the largest military and paramilitary force on Earth. This combination of forces amounts to 5,889,000 people. This is 25 percent of the entire population of North Korea, another statistic that is unmatched throughout the world. No other country has 25 percent of its entire population in the military services. The KPA, or Korean People's Army, consists of five branches: ground force, the navy, the air force, the strategic rocket forces, and the special operations force. They also have the Worker-Peasant Red Guards. Available for military service is age seventeen. Japan ruled Korea from 1910 until the last days of World War II. In an agreement with the United States, the Soviet Union was given the territory north of the thirty-eighth parallel, and the US forces occupied the south. By 1948 Korea was split into two regions with separate governments. Both the United States and the Soviet Union claimed to be the legitimate government of all of Korea. Just after World War II and during the Soviet Union's occupation of the part of Korea north of the thirty-eighth parallel, the Soviet army's twenty-fifth division headquarters in Pyongyang issued a statement ordering all armed men of resistance groups to disband on October 12,1945. Formation of a new unit was activated on August 15 to create a national armed guard. The Korean People's Army was founded by the KPA military academy in December 1948 and soon followed with education of political and military officers for the new armed forces. The units became military regulars with distribution of Soviet uniforms, badges, and weapons. On June 25,1950, seventy-five thousand forces from the KPA smashed into South Korea, setting off the Korean War. The North Korean forces surprised the South Korean Army and a small US force that was stationed in the country at the time. On June 27 the United Nations Security council authorized the formation and dispatch of UN forces to Korea. This action was to repel the North Korean invasion. Twenty-one countries contributed to the UN force, but the United States provided 88 percent of the military personnel. After two years of war, the US forces were on the edge of defeat. They were forced into a small area in the south known as the Pusan Perimeter. In September 1950, a UN counter-offensive was launched at Incheon. It was an amphibious landing by mainly US troops. It was effective because it cut off many North Korean troops. Those who were not killed or captured were forced to flee back to North Korea. UN forces approached the Yalu River, which borders China, but by October 1950, masses of Chinese troops crossed the river into Korea and entered the war. The surprise Chinese intervention caused the retreat of the UN forces, and Seoul changed hands four times. In the last two years of the war, it became a war of attrition with a stalemate and most of the front line close to the thirty-eighth parallel. The fighting has stopped, but there has been no formal treaty signed to declare the war officially over. Technically the war is still going on but with a cease-fire in place. The North Koreans officially call the war the "Fatherland Liberation War." In China they still call the Korean War the "War to Resist US Aggression." In the United States, the war was described as an undeclared military action by the United Nations.

So where do we go from here? Some people believe that Kim Jong-un has been planning to attack the United States for years. North Korea shows no sign of stopping its nuclear program or slowing down in its progress on intercontinental ballistic missiles (ICBMs). North Korea has progressed to the point where it now scares the entire world with a nuclear global threat. Should we really count on China to intervene? It was China and the former Soviet Union that liberated North Korea and have protected this region. Kim Jong-un is possibly the biggest real threat to US safety. There is no comparison between ISIS and North Korea. North Korea has a real army; real navy; real air force; and short-range, long-range ICBM rockets to attack Japan, South Korea, China, Malaysia, and even the United States. ISIS and its imported terrorists to the United States can cause havoc and kill perhaps hundreds within our country, but North Korea may cause millions of Americans to perish from the earth. The ICBM program in North Korea made huge strides in 2016. This year (2017) has now the North Koreans making greater strides. It was estimated in early 2016 that North Korea would not have a working, effective ICBM until 2021. Now these estimates are moved up to perhaps the next eight months. The biggest challenge to the success of an ICBM is reentry into Earth's atmosphere. It is hard to keep the warhead on target while it is moving at hypersonic speeds, when friction with the air forms a shroud of superheated plasma around the reentry vehicle. Whatever material burns away from the heat shield must do so in a uniform, symmetric manner. Kim Jong-un recently examined a North Korean reentry vehicle that seemed to indicate uniform ablation at the conclusion of the test, according to photos released by the North Korean government. The rocket, the KN-14, could reach California. It has been shown in parades but not flight tested. David Wright, missile expert from the Union of Concerned Scientists, says that "the paraded KN-14 can be seen to have two stages. This indicates that liquid fuel is used rather than a solid fuel is being used." Although liquid fuel requires relatively heavy pumping systems, it tends to be better at lifting mass. And, with fewer stages, there is less potential for complications. Our scientists can detect the propellant being used by simply observing the exhaust. In the earlier tests, the North Koreans had a smoky exhaust, indicating kerosene, but the recent plume has been orange in color, indicating carbon, and translucent. This would indicate unsymmetrical dimethyl hydrazine. This mixture would also give the rocket 15 percent more power, says Dr. Schilling. Schilling also stated, "It was more advanced and efficient than anything we had really expected them to be able to develop for the first stage of their ICBMs." US experts surmise that North Koreans placed nuclear warheads on short-range missiles back in 2013. That same technology can be used on an ICBM. "Most North Korean nuclear-capable missiles seem to have a payload section about 65 centimeters in diameter, appropriate for a first-generation warhead," Schilling says. Some people claim that North Korea could destroy South Korea, Japan, and a major part of China with the nuclear weapons they already possess and that the United States could sit back because the North Korean missiles could not reach the United States at this time, but that is not true. Kim Jong–un's ICBMs may be incapable at this time of reaching

California with reentry from space, but the shorter- and medium-range missiles could be hidden inside a freighter ship in the middle of the ocean or off the California coast. This kind of attack would not be a terrorist attack from North Korea; it would be a full-blown nuclear attack, killing millions in the United States. The US intelligence services do not know how many operational nukes the North Koreans have. Make no mistake, the North Koreans will not stop in their production of nukes or their quest to be in a position to launch a very deadly and devastating attack against their main enemy, which is the United States. North Korea also has an advanced military and highly trained soldiers, sailors, and airmen. One of the fears that keeps our own navy up at night are underwater missions and frogmen who could wreak havoc on our naval ships. Lately there have been detections of ghosts in the water. I am talking about scuba divers. The United States' Navy SEALs are not the only divers around the world. Russia, England, China, Japan, India…and North Korea. The United States has growing concerns of major conflicts erupting in Asia, Africa, the Middle East, and beyond; there is a rise in special operations missions near the seaports of some of the biggest militaries around the globe. Recently the Chinese claimed they were threatened by a Japanese naval ship that sent divers to approach a Chinese warship while it was docked at Djibouti. This drama unfolded in eastern Africa, which is far away from both countries' home shores. The Japanese military did not report the incident. But Jian Jiamin, a legal counselor with China's PLA navy who served in Africa, reported the encounter to the media. These underwater encounters are rarely detected. As a hypothetical example, the US Navy should be very wary of the Naval Station in Norfolk, Virginia. A high alert would be reasonable, considering there are more than sixty ships docked at that naval base, including the newest *USS Ford* aircraft carrier. These are some of our nation's military assets, and it would be a tremendous loss if these ships were sabotaged or blown up with explosives. There is an underwater security gate that encircles the fourteen piers at Norfolk. This gate was built by Halo Maritime Defense company. Perhaps that would be a good choice to also assist with the border wall. Many critics have said you can't build a border wall over water; well, Maritime Defense can do it. The fences are designed to keep out small boats and terrorists, but they would not really stop professional divers. Frogmen pose special threats, and sophisticated warships are very wary of them. Divers can do two things very well: sabotage the harbor itself and the vessels, and they can collect intelligence. The frogmen could be scouting future missions or installing equipment that could cause damage at a later date. They can plant microphones inside the port and record the activity of the ships. They can determine the amount of fuel they are getting and what kind of weapons the ships are carrying. There are often fiber-optic umbilical lines between the pier and the ship that could be tapped. The US Navy piers also use wireless connection systems, and those signals could also be intercepted. A carefully planned plot from perhaps North Korean divers could really be a disaster, especially using explosives. The last time a frogman hit a United States ship was in 1964. It was a single Vietnamese diver who sank the *USS Card* with an explosive attached to the hull. The same threat surfaced almost forty years later when the US military discovered the plot of Abd al-Rahim al-Nashiri, the same mastermind of Al Qaeda's deadly suicide boat attack on the *USS Cole*, which killed dozens of US Navy servicemen. Nashiri also trained numerous recruits to plant explosives under docked ships in the Persian Gulf. Other advantages of using frogmen to carry out attacks is these frogmen don't have to be attached to a ship to blow it up. They could make improvised underwater mines or even use ones that they can purchase on the black market.

How has a nation like North Korea advanced these deadly technologies when it has been so isolated?

North Korea has collaborated with Iran and Pakistan, developing nuclear and/or missile technology in the past, and evidence suggests that this may be ongoing. It has received assistance from Russia in technical and most likely military personnel during the Boris Yeltsen years. For a good five years, the Soviet army members were not being paid salaries due to Soviet Union shortfalls in their national budget. The former Soviet Union was not able to track what its military scientists were doing on the side. We know that Russian military personnel worked for Muammar Gaddafi of Libya, Saddam Hussein of Iraq, and, of course, extensively with Iran, all to make up for that lack of money from Russia. Secondhand missiles from Egypt and Syria could have been reverse engineered. Missile transporters from China and technology from Ukraine have also been reported. North Korea is a minor industrial power but it spends over 25 percent of its entire gross domestic product on defense. In this case it is not military defense but military offense. This dedication to a massive missile and military budget is now at the expense of its own people. The people of North Korea are almost suffering from mass starvation. Reports out of the country report that the peasant farmers and everyday workers have a diet of eating dirt, tree bark and deprived of basic nutrition

CHAPTER 10

Congress: Throw Them All Out and Lock the Door!

I AM NOT EVEN SURE where to start on this subject. Felony and misdemeanor convictions, sex crimes, insider trading, conflicts of interest, trading votes for favors, increasing their power base through strong-arm tactics, keeping the old guard in power, and just downright corruption is what is going on in Washington every single day. These are the activities of the United States House of Representatives and the United States Senate. The love of power and the love of money have created a climate where backstabbing and corruption is the norm and not the exception. Politicians no longer go to Washington, DC, to just represent their districts or states. They now go to Washington, DC, to make politics a business venture. They go to get rich. They don't live *for* politics; they live *off* politics. Most of them enter with a modest net worth, especially if they have never worked in the private sector. These individuals, over time, may end up multimillionaires. Reuters on March 13, 2008, ran a story titled "Get Elected to Congress and Get Rich." It was Interesting what happened just before the Obama term in office when the members of Congress were so outspoken and concerned about the 2008–09 mortgage and stock market meltdown where Americans lost trillions in home values and the stock market. At the same time, members of Congress actually gained an estimated net worth of 6 percent during the same time frame while the rest of the country was down 23 percent.

Insider stock trading is legal if you are an elected politician. Remember, insider stock trading is what Martha Stewart went to prison for! Members of Congress can trade stocks based on privileged information that is unavailable to the general public. I believe it was Al Capone who said, "I don't play the stock market; it is a rigged game." Yes, it is rigged, especially if someone has direct knowledge of government contracts and government projects that are yet to be awarded to American or foreign businesses. The classic example would be a Pentagon contract. If someone from Congress is sitting on the Armed Forces Committee, he or she is now aware which firms are bidding for military hardware or equipment. He or she also will know or approve which company gets the job. Almost always the company that gets the contract will increase its corporate revenue and company profitability. When that happens the common stock price will rise. In some cases, the common stock can go up substantially. You can guess what happens next. The members of Congress on that committee will purchase the stock in their own accounts before the announcement of the contract being finalized with the Pentagon. Everyone on the committee gets rich, especially if he or she bought the stock on a margin account or acquired "call option contracts." Consequently, for the companies that were not as lucky to be awarded the government contract, their stock tends to fall in price when an announcement is made that the contract was awarded to another competitor. Again, the members of Congress can and would benefit by purchasing "put option contracts" or even selling the "stock short" to double down on the gain. Remember, they already made a gain on the stock price rising and can also make a gain with the stocks of the other companies that failed to get the contracts and then go down in price. The rest of us go to jail for doing these transactions based on insider trading, but not so for members of Congress. If you think that is all unfair, this next revelation is where the good part begins. The members of the US House and Senate do have relationships with each other and in many cases have numerous friendships. Contrary to what you see on the nightly news or on television, the insults and disagreements between Democrats and Republicans are often exaggerated, and they are "putting on an act" for their voters to be satisfied.

Having said that, these Congressional committee members talk to each other. Perhaps a conversation would go like this. John (the Senate Democrat) says, "I see your panel is meeting this afternoon to award the construction contract on seven new airports being upgraded and refurbished in several states. I hope it is going well."

"Yes it is," states Tim, the Senator from Nebraska on the committee.

"Well, you know, I sit on the Public transportation Committee, and we are choosing new railway contractors for fourteen different cities next week. If you tell me who is going to get your committee contract, then I don't mind sharing who we are going to appoint for the rail programs." Sharing insider information to keep favors going and to keep up their power base is commonplace in the House and the Senate. House speaker Nancy Pelosi and her husband, Paul Pelosi, made three purchases of Visa stock between $1 million and $5 million. They were able to buy an IPO (initial public offering stock). The IPO was Visa stock and had been privately held stock by a group of different banks. If you have ever purchased an IPO from your stockbroker, you would know that in most cases, the number of shares you can get are very limited. If the offering is popular, it will be labeled oversubscribed, and it will be called a hot issue. Firms in the have been Tesla, Apple, and Google, to name a few. Pelosi and her husband acquired those shares—and $5 million is not a few shares—just two weeks after a piece of legislation was introduced in the House of Representatives that would hurt Visa in its ability to maintain higher credit card fees. The name of the bill being introduced was the Credit Card Fair Free Act of 2008. The bill would have allowed retailers to negotiate lower fees with Visa and other credit-card countries. Pelosi is the kind of lawmaker who would normally back something that would help the little guy, the consumer. The backers of the bill lobbied for a vote, but it never happened. Pelosi never asked for the hearing on the house floor, so the bill died. If you get the picture, Nancy made a deal with Visa. The deal was: I will kill the bill if you get me the ability to buy the stock before the trading begins. When the trading begins, then anyone can buy or sell anytime.

Insider deals in the area of real-estate transactions are even more prevalent, and they have been larger transactions but are easier to camouflage than stock deals. The stock deals happen faster, and the Securities and Exchange Commission (SEC) keeps records of stock trades. The land deals can take years. One of the more exposed real-estate deals was with the former Republican speaker of the House Dennis Hastert in 2004. On July 31, 2002, Kirk Brown approved a land corridor for a road named the Prairie Parkway in Kendall County, Illinois. Prior to the approval, Hastert bought a 195-acre farm on Little Rock Creek in Illinois. The farm was around two miles from the new proposed parkway. Hastert, with two partners, bought more land in 2004. They bought sixty-nine acres, and they paid $15,000 per acre. In one transaction alone, Hastert who had a trust called the Little Rock Trust, transferred sixty-nine acres to that trust. The trust was owned by him and his wife. Months later, a little more than a year he made the purchase of land, he was able to sell the land for $4.9 million. So the profit was 140 percent—the land sold for $36,000 an acre.

Nancy and Paul Pelosi have also, over the years, made big gains in real estate. Pelosi, as speaker of the House, has secured federal monies for many projects on behalf of the city of San Francisco. One of these projects is the Third Street Light Rail project. The Third Street project is one of the most expensive light rail projects ever built, costing taxpayers $660 million for a six-mile route. Pelosi got the start-up funding to the tune of $532 million. She also got another $200 million to keep this project going. The transit line helps revitalize the San Francisco neighborhood. A few blocks from the light rail is a building owned by Paul and Nancy Pelosi. The four-story office building they own is worth around $5 million today, but their sharp rise in profit from paying less than $1 million originally is directly connected to the transportation line. Senator Chuck Schumer owns commercial buildings in New York and has done similar insider positioning. The Clintons own commercial buildings, and Hillary sponsored legislation while she was a senator from New York that made the Clintons big profits.

Who are the richest US congressmen and senators?

1. Congressman Darrel Issa, Republican from California, is considered the richest US congressman. His estimated wealth is in the $464 million range. He was elected to his ninth term in 2016; however, his political office influence had little to do with his wealth. Most of the wealth was amassed during his time as CEO of Directed Electronics, an auto parts and accessories company.
2. Senator Mark Warner, Democrat from Virginia, was elected in 2009 and served as the state's governor from 2002 to 2006. Warner's net worth is estimated at $257.5 million. Warner was an early investor in cellphone technology.
3. Congressman Jared Polis, Democrat from Colorado, was first elected in 2008. He is also the only openly gay parent to serve in Congress. His estimated net worth is around $200 million. He founded American Information Systems while in college and also founded other companies like Proflowers.com.
4. Congressman John Delaney, Democrat from Maryland, has an estimated net worth of $155 million.
5. Congressman Michael McCaul, Republican from Texas, has an estimated net worth of $143 million. First elected in 2005.
6. Congressman Scott Peters from California, Democrat. His estimated net worth is $112.5 million.
7. Senator Richard Blumenthal, Democrat from Connecticut, has an estimated net worth of $104 million. Blumenthal was a classmate of both Bill and Hillary Clinton at Yale University.
8. Congresswoman Nancy Pelosi from California, Democrat, became the highest-ranking female politician in the country's history when she served as speaker of the House between 2007 and 2011. She also

was the only former or current speaker of the House to demand that an Air Force One presidential jet be assigned to her and her staff members. This cost the US taxpayers the highest travel budget of all time. Pelosi's net worth is estimated at $100 million.
9. Senator Diane Feinstein, Democrat from California, has been a US senator since 1992. For twenty-five years she has been sitting on several important committees. Feinstein is a Stanford graduate. She actually ran for governor of California in 1990 and lost to Peter Wilson. She has an estimated net worth of $75 million.

"Pay to Play" is a term now used often in the press. The MSM has used the term even in describing the Clinton Foundation. Does that name fit, and can you make a case that the Clinton Foundation accepted donations for favors? The answer is 100 percent yes. The Clinton Foundation actually received a direct donation from Russia. The real Russian government. Why would the Russians give a US-based charitable organization a donation? The answer is that the Russians would receive a favor in return. The favor in this case was Hillary giving them a buy-in of 25 percent of our uranium reserves. This was arranged while she was the secretary of state. The Russians gave her campaign manager, John Pedestal, direct monies before Hillary ran for the nomination of POTUS. Even her husband, Bill Clinton, got inflated speaking fees from the Russians. All of these events are examples of "pay to play."

One of the biggest pay-to-play examples was during the "Obama for President" campaign. The pay to play was a federally backed low-interest loan. If the company could not make enough profits to pay the loan back, the federal government would step in and make up the shortfall. It was a taxpayer-backed loan. Solyndra was a green energy company making solar panels. Obama visited the factory, which was located in California, twice. The company has never been profitable, and it lost money on its solar panel sales from the get-go. So here is where the pay to play comes in. The largest owner of Solyndra company stock was a billionaire from Oklahoma. He name is George Kaiser. George Kaiser was one of the largest fundraisers for the Obama 2008 campaign. Kaiser collected a minimum of $100,000 from each contributor, and he was able to collectively get numerous friends and associates to each give the $100,000. This would mean millions for the Obama campaign. This is a classic example of pay to play. In this example, "If you donate and help me get elected, I will give you taxpayer dollars to kick off your business venture—sounds good to me!"

Why Don't They Ever Leave?
How long should these lawmakers be allowed to stay in government service? Many of them, like Governors Gerry Brown of California and John Kasich, are career politicians. In the case of John Kasich, he began his involvement or desire for politics in1970 when he met President Richard Nixon at the White House. Kasich was a freshman at Ohio State University, and his visit was as a private citizen. John Kasich had written a letter to President Nixon but first gave the letter to the acting president of Ohio State University, president Novice Fawcett. Fawcett then sent it on to the White House, and Kasich had a twenty-minute meeting with President Richard Nixon. The letter was about Kasich's concerns over the direction of the United States at the time. Keep in mind, this was height of the war in Vietnam. After Kasich graduated from college with a bachelor of arts in political science in 1974, it did not take him long to begin his career in politics. After graduating in 1974, he worked for the Ohio State Legislative Commission and then as an aide to State Senator Buzz Lukens up until 1978. In 1978 he ran for the Ohio senate, representing the fifteenth district. Kasich was the youngest person ever elected to the Ohio Senate at age twenty-six. In 1982 Kasich ran for US Congress, representing the twelfth district; he was reelected eight times, spending eighteen years in Congress from 1983 to 2001. Kasich did leave Congress in 2001 but basically as a commentator for the Fox News Channel; he hosted a show called *Heartland with John Kasich* and guest-hosted *The O'Reilly Factor* and *Hannity & Colmes*. The most money he ever made was when Lehman Bros hired him as a managing director in Columbus, Ohio. The year Lehman Brothers declared bankruptcy, Kasich was paid a $182,692 salary and a $432,200 bonus.

This reinforces the above facts about politicians or former politicians; they make money even when the rest of us lose money. In 2008 Kasich formed a political action committee that raised money for Republican candidates. In 2010 Kasich ran for governor of Ohio against incumbent Democrat Ted Strickland. Kasich won the vote in a close race. In 2019 John Kasich finally will have to step away from the governor's office due to term limits; he will be sixty-eight years old. Will he run for US Senate, or would he even make another run for president of the United States? Only time will tell, but Kasich has spent his entire adult life in politics—forty-three years and two more to go for a total of forty-five years. If he runs for Ohio senate and wins in 2020, he will be pushing fifty-one years in politics.

Governor Gerry Brown is not far behind Kasich and actually has been in politics or around politics his entire adult life. Born in San Francisco on April 7, 1938, Brown is seventy-eight years old. His real name is Edmund Gerald Brown, and he is the current governor of California, the most populous state in the United States. Jerry is highly educated, receiving his undergraduate degree from University of California at Berkeley and his doctor of laws degree at Yale University. Brown was first elected governor in 1974 at age thirty-six, the youngest California governor in 111 years. Before that he was California's secretary of state from 1971 to 1975. Brown actually began his political career as a member of the Los Angeles Community College District Board of Trustees from 1969 to 1971. He ran for the Democratic Party presidential election in 1976, finishing second in the popular vote and a distant third in the convention vote, losing to Jimmy Carter. Brown was reelected California governor in 1978 but even ran against Jimmy Carter in the 1980 primaries. Carter had low approval ratings, and United States citizens had been held captive in Iran for over one year. This captivity did not sit well with the American people at the time. Brown lost again to Carter, and Carter was soundly defeated by Ronald Reagan. Brown ran again for US Senate in 1982 but was defeated by Pete Wilson. Brown served as the chairman of the California Democratic Party from 1989 to 1991 and then ran for the Democratic nomination for president again in 1992, once again coming in second behind Governor Bill

Clinton of Arkansas. After six years out of politics, Brown ran for mayor of Oakland; he won and served from 1999 to 2007. Brown went on to become the attorney general of California from 2007 to 2011. Finally, he ran again against Republican Meg Whitman in 2010 to become the thirty-ninth California governor. Due to his first term as California governor back in 1974, on October 7, 2013, Brown became the longest-serving governor in California history. Brown had a gap of twenty-eight years between his second and third terms. He has the distinction of being the sixth-youngest California governor and the oldest California governor in history. So if you add up all the years in politics (taking six years off to travel around the United States and abroad), Brown will have been in politics for fifty-five years. Brown could run for president of the United States in 2020, but he would be eighty-two years old. Another run would also be the fourth time he has tried to get elected for POTUS. "Never say never, Jerry."

Other career politicians who never leave office include some in the House and the Senate:

1. John Dingell, fifty-seven years
2. Daniel Inouye, fifty-three years
3. John Conyers, fifty years
4. Charles Rangel, forty-eight years
5. Thad Cochran, forty-four years
6. Pete Stark, forty-four years
7. Bill Young, forty-four years
8. Chuck Schumer, thirty-six years
9. John McCain, thirty-six years
10. Nancy Pelosi, twenty-nine years

If passing new legislation is the question, then the Republicans are the problem!

The Republicans should be called "the gang that couldn't shoot straight," or a better description on their failures might be, "The Republicans would screw up a *one*-car funeral." Republicans have said over and over, "If we could have the majority in US House and the Senate, we will repeal and replace Obamacare, aka the Affordable Care Act." The ACA is now an oxymoron because this health care is not affordable. The Republicans also said, in 2011, "We will give the American people a tax reform bill, aka a 'tax cut,' and we will give American businesses a tax cut." So fast forward to 2015 and leading up to November 2016, the Republicans said, "If we can win the White House, then we can get all our items done, such as: repeal and replace Obamacare, tax reform bill, immigration reform, and begin reducing the national debt of the United States." As of July 20, 2017, following a full six months of the Trump presidency and having a majority voting advantage in both the House and the Senate for the same time period, there has been no progress and no legislation passed on any of these items.

What is their problem? Is it because they are incompetent? Is it because they do not present a united front? Is it because it is not in their best interests? Is it because they could lose votes? Is it because they are lazy? Is it because some of them want Trump to fail? The answer is all of the above. Next time around, with the 2018 midterm elections and the 2020 elections, I hope Americans study some of the issues and proposed, pending legislation. All Americans should look at their representatives and see how they are voting and see how they are going to vote in the future. Many elected politicians say one thing and do another, especially when it comes to the media. Colluding with the media is the favorite pastime of the Democrats, in the last few years—but don't be fooled, the Republicans do it also. Senator John McCain has leaked several stories against Trump that were not accurate. John McCain and Senator Lindsey Graham have been the most active. They have also have colluded most often with media who write and report harmful stories. Democrats and Republicans are pushing the MSM buttons to produce stories that help their agenda, and if these stories hurt others, then all the better.

If the pattern over the past forty-eight years continues, then the Trump administration is in for a rocky road ahead. The numbers are not on his side.

Someone should have told Donald that Republicans do get in hot water from time to time. In fact, you could say they get in hot water most of the time. Why can't the Republicans who work in the executive branch stay out of jail? Most people will be shocked at the number of administration employees who have worked for Republican administrations who have been indicted, convicted, and even gone to prison. Below is a comparison between the two parties over time. Keep in mind these numbers do not include members of Congress. When it comes to Congress, Republicans and Democrats are about even. So far, during the Trump administration, three have been convicted: Congressman Anthony Weiner, Democrat; Congresswoman Corrine Brown, Democrat; and Congressman Greg Giantorie, Republican. I might add, though, Weiner and Brown are going to prison for multiple years for serious crimes, and Giantorie received probation.

Executive Branch Past Forty-Eight Years: Indictments, Convictions, Prison

Average Indictments Per Year	Average Convictions Per Year	Years in Power
Republicans 4.29	Republicans 3.18	28 years
Democrats 0.15	Democrats 0.05	20 years

Total Indictments	Total Convictions	Total Prison Sentences
Republicans 120	Republicans 89	34
Democrats 3	Democrats 1	1

Indictments per POTUS

1. Obama: 0
2. Bush "W": 16
3. Clinton: 2
4. Bush H. W.: 1
5. Reagan: 26
6. Carter: 1
7. Nixon: 76

A warning to Trump: these numbers above illustrate it is a "rigged game," and many Democrats should have been indicted who were not touched because Obama controlled the Department of Justice where the indictments would come from. Names like Hillary Clinton, John Podesta, Lois Learner, Eric Holder, Susan Rice, Sheryl Mills, and others should all be indicted. General Petraeus was convicted of much lesser crimes and punished. The Democrats stick together and defend their own. On the other hand, the Republicans do not defend their own. That is why Trump is not being better protected by his own Republican party. It is time to call out all these bad actors. Republicans and Democrats are self-serving and need to stop spending so much time in front of the television cameras; instead, they should spend more time at the Capitol building in their chambers. Stay in their chambers so they can get the real job done for the American people—otherwise, throw 'em all out!

Perhaps it is time to pass the Twenty-Eighth Amendment to the Constitution: "Congress shall make no law that applies to the citizens of the United States that does not apply equally to the Senators and/or House Representatives; and Congress shall make no law that applies to the Senators and/or Representatives that does not apply equally to the citizens of the United States." Below is a partial list of the unfair and abusive conditions that currently exist:

1. The children of Congress members do not have to pay back their college student loans.
2. Staffers of Congress and their family members do not have to pay back their college student loans.
3. Members of Congress can retire at full salary after only one term served. They also get annual cost of living increases every year for life.
4. Members of Congress are exempt from many laws that would be felony crimes for the rest of us regular Americans. This exemption is especially true in the area of financial crimes, where insider trading is allowed for congressmen and senators. They also get away with "pay to play," which is an activity that would pass new legislation by

a Senator or Congressman when the result is rewarding their congressional district financially by numerous methods.
5. They have exempted themselves from the current health-care laws under Obamacare, and at this point they get special insurance coverage because they are members of Congress.

Governors of thirty-five states have filed suit against the US federal government for imposing these elite advantages and unlawful burdens upon the United States. It only takes thirty-eight governors out of the fifty states to convene a Constitutional convention.

CHAPTER 11

The Border Wall

TRUMP CAME UP WITH THE border wall idea and raised eyebrows when he said Mexico would pay for it. The liberals were outraged. Why would someone say that? Why do we need a wall that would be a real wall and effective enough in keeping people out of US territory? The real facts are that for thousands of years, border and territory walls have been built and defended throughout the civilized world. The only geographical exceptions were the vast American and Canadian territories occupied by Eskimos, Native American Indians, the Aboriginals of Australia, the Zulu tribes of Africa, and the Arab nomads of the Persian and Sahara deserts. The Great Wall of China was built to keep the Mongolian warlords and the northerners from attacking the Chinese; the wall was also defended for a thousand years. When it was finally completed, it was 13,000 miles in length. Hadrian's 135-kilometer wall was constructed by the Romans before the birth of Christ and completed in AD 128; it took them almost 150 years of building to keep the savage people, now the country of Scotland, out of the Roman-occupied territory of England. They were called the Pics, and they were fierce fighters. The Romans were a bit bothered by the Pics. Romans considered the Pics complete savages. The Pics painted themselves blue from head to toe, and they fought naked. Old Roman stories speak of their savage behavior, and I am sure the Roman soldiers who were sent to fight the Pics all suffered from PTSD, posttraumatic stress disorder. Regardless of the Roman victories, the Romans could not keep the Pics from wandering back into English territory and attacking Roman garrisons. Scotland and the former Pics occupied the only territory in the vast Roman Empire that was never actually conquered or ruled by Rome. When the Romans started a campaign to invade and occupy a territory, they were 100 percent successful, except for the territory of Scotland. Both the Great Wall of China and Hadrian's Wall still stand today.

What are the other countries doing when it comes to border walls? A third of the world's countries have or are building border walls. In 1989 when the Berlin Wall was torn down, there were only twelve walls to protect national borders; today, sixty-five countries are building and increasing their border security, and seventy walls now exist. After suffering a series of terrorist attacks, the Tunisian government had enough when they had the slaughter of more than three dozen mostly British tourists in the beach resort town of Sousse. Tunisia has built a wall that is 200 kilometers or 125 miles long, between Tunisia and Libya. Libya is still in a civil war, and the danger to Tunisia is out of control. The wall is three meters high and has barbed wire at the top. Their wall also has trenches and they have also built an earth wall. The border wall between Turkey and Syria consists of concrete slabs topped with razor wire. The border wall built by the country of India to separate it from Bangladesh has barriers lower to the ground, layered with posts, wire fences, and rolls of barbed wire. The Israel–West Bank wall is very high, and it consists of narrow concrete slabs topped with wire fencing. Fences and walls are going up everywhere, and believe it or not, the walls are actually increasing in their effectiveness, and they are becoming a priority ever since Trump began his dialogue on the subject of building a wall.

There are no reports of any countries actually tearing down any border walls. India's 2,500-mile fence around Bangladesh is being built to keep those from Bangladesh out of India. In Israel fortified walls are built around cities. Israel has the "apartheid" wall, also a formidable wall, on the border between Israel and Palestine. Austria is another country now defending its border against the Italian territory, where thousands of Syrian refugees are crossing the Mediterranean Sea into Italy and then trying to get to Germany and other European countries. Hungary is building a 110-mile-long wall to separate it from Serbia. Turkey is constructing a five-hundred-mile wall along its southern border to repel the Syrian refugees. Sweden, Denmark, and Switzerland have extensive guarded borders, and so does Germany.

Mexico has not yet paid for the US-Mexico border wall as of the published date of this book. But it doesn't really matter if they pay or not. The fact that Trump alone came up with the idea of having Mexico pay for the wall was genius for his campaign, and it resonated with many people in the United States. Open borders and mass immigration had created fear for safety, fear of prosperity, and quality of life for many Americans. The Hillary Clinton POTUS campaign ignored this fact, and so did the Democrats. This was a catastrophic miscalculation on their part. It became a campaign issue, and the argument for border security was proved correct when Trump won the election.

Technology has improved over the past few years, to say the least, and so have new inventions. The questions surrounding the border wall will continue to be: How effective is this wall going to be, and what will it cost? When the ancient walls were built over two thousand years ago, in some cases, the effectiveness came down to two factors: Was the wall high enough so the enemies could not go over the top, and could it be defended by garrisons or troops mounted on to top or even inside the wall itself?

Our border wall with Mexico has a much different task and specific cause of action. We are not fighting warriors or attackers with hordes of armies. We are deterring migrants, drug smugglers, human traffickers, and even those seeking work by entering the country illegally. This would require that the wall be impassable but also monitored in case it was breached.

The cons of mass immigration far outweigh the pros. It goes without saying that logic must take over, and in the end, logic will win every time. As Americans we must look at some point to what is described as limited resources. Limited resources means limited water, food, housing, open lands, and energy. Then we have the byproducts of overcrowding and overpopulation, for example, increased crime, increased traffic, congestion, increased pollution, airline travel delays due to increased travelers. Natural population growth is about all we can stand unless we seek a drop in quality of life.

There is a wide set of arguments, for or against, the increased construction and additional cost of the border wall. Many Americans fought overseas to actually help other countries so their countries could be a safer place. In doing that, Americans paid a sacrifice. Lives were lost, and families were heartbroken at the loss of loved ones. Not to mention the injuries to those wounded warriors, losing limbs, eyesight, hearing loss, and suffering from PTSD. Many families ask the question: How much longer will we have to support the entire world and all their problems? Do we really owe the world? This is the great debate in the United States. Save the world! or America first! that is the question.

I have heard many good-hearted people say, "I consider myself a world citizen, not just a United States citizen." The people in that camp will accept the belief that if we do not take in refugees, mainly from war-torn countries, then who will? Others, mainly the Trumpeters, take a different attitude, and their thinking lies in protecting what we have built and established as a better quality of life that we enjoy in America versus other countries. Both points can be well taken. The right to protect our borders should not be debated. In today's world there are stronger reasons for border security. Border security creates a more manageable society and freedom to keep and improve a lifestyle that breeds off the successes of our country. There is an old saying: "If it ain't broke, why fix it?" In the United States, it should be known to all that other cultures are now rapidly moving to places all over the globe. This is good in some ways for parts of the world, and it also has been a disaster in other places like England, Germany, Sweden, and France. The specific cultures that wish to change the way we live in the United States and not disseminate must be watched closely, and if they are too aggressive or persistent in this quest, we must stop it or make sure we are not compromised. I refer to the Muslim sharia. Sharia will not and should not be tolerated in the United States under any circumstances. If the borders are left unprotected, and if immigration is not enforced, then the masses will enter the United States. When an overwhelming number of one particular group is allowed to colonize, then the community becomes overrun and even taken over. If a community is overrun, and they do not assimilate within the region, then a whole new culture forms in that country or that area. In the case of Muslim sharia values, this is not a new culture. Sharia is an ancient culture that is a complete throwback to medieval days and totally unfair to women and non-Muslims. What culture would punish and even kill others who disagree with their beliefs? The absurdity of that is just unreal in today's society.

The Canada/United States border is the longest border in the entire world. The border is 8,893 kilometers long. So why don't we have a wall to protect us from Canada? I think that is really a trick question. Are we afraid of massive moose crossings? Perhaps we could experience rabid hockey fans who want to invade. Many people place Canada on a pedestal. This is just a nice, clean country, and they have very low crime. For the variety of reasons I just mentioned, a border wall has not been constructed, and neither has a fence been constructed to separate the two countries. It should be said Canada might not exist if it could not trade with the United States. Canada is very dependent on the United States. For the most part there are border-crossing checkpoints and border security at each checkpoint. The area is so vast that driving across the US-Canadian border would just be done with an off-road vehicle, and in many places, roads do cross over the US-Canada border with no checkpoints in the very remote locations. The situation at the US-Canada border is really the opposite of the Mexico-United States border wall. The first reason is that it is the opposite situation: Americans are leaving America to go to Canada. The Canadians are not flocking to the United States to live here. So the United States does not need big protection from the horde of Canadians coming into the United States. The second reason the Canadians don't need a wall is because Americans or people from any other countries cannot stay in Canada very long. The Canadians will kick you out if you try to overstay your welcome. Canada provides free health care and other services. They will monitor the people who try to use these services without proper papers and proof of citizenship. Work permits are required and also monitored for noncitizens. Canada has a no-nonsense policy on deportations, except for asylum-seekers or refugees allowed in under a Canadian compassion rule.

Trump will be judged harshly if the US-Mexico border wall is not constructed. It must go up within his first term in office, or there may not be a second term for Trump. The American people will remember how Trump spoke about the border wall, and he said with so much confidence, "I am a great builder, and this is no problem for me." I believe the border wall needs to be constructed as a great wall and not an imaginary wall. Trump will let his people down and his voters down if he does not build a wall that stands out visually and is imposing. Trump must back up that he is the self-proclaimed great builder, and he will need to accomplish a great wall. The MSM conversation, and among many weak Republicans, has become more negative to building a physical wall. They are now saying is not possible based on the terrain. The MSM keeps inflating the cost of the wall. So bids have come in from contractors as low as $2 billion and as high as $33 billion. In contrast, the California high-speed rail project, which will take passengers from Anaheim, California, to San Francisco, California, will cost an $64 billion, but that was in 2012 when the project was approved. The cost was actually escalated to $98 billion when extension tracks were added to have the train travel to San Diego and also to Sacramento, California. The train project has been scaled back to just going from Palmdale to the San Francisco train station; now the cost is predicted to be $68 billion. The high-speed train is supposed to travel at 220 miles per hour, and with zero stops, it could arrive in two hours forty-nine minutes. It will have stops in central California, so the trip will be around three hours if the train can actually travel that fast. The high-speed train is currently the largest public works project in the United States and by far the most expensive. Most experts are predicting a $100 billion final cost as opposed to the $68 billion estimate. They also predict delays that will take the final completion date somewhere out until 2029. According to a May 12,

2015, study done by the *Los Angeles Times*, the current project fare will be eighty-six dollars one way per passenger. By the way, a few facts on the high-speed rail project. The first service will begin at Palmdale, California, and that is a good hour away from downtown Los Angeles and two hours away if one is driving during rush hour. From there the route carries passengers to Bakersfield, Tulare, Fresno Madera, Gilroy, San Jose Millbrae/SFO airport, and finally to San Francisco. The Palmdale start point is estimated to be completed by 2025. Sometime in 2029, the high-speed train will go into the Los Angeles basin and arrive in Anaheim, California. The fact is, most of those who commute to San Francisco from the Los Angeles basin will never use that train. Why would you drive two hours to get on a train that will take three more hours to get you to San Francisco when you can fly in one hour? There are three surrounding airports located in the San Francisco Bay area. There is San Francisco International airport eighteen minutes from the city; Oakland International Airport, which is thirty minutes from the city of San Francisco; and finally there is San Jose International Airport, which is forty minutes from the city of San Francisco. It all comes down to the great divide between liberals versus conservatives with their ongoing debates in the United States today between projects that are going to bankrupt our country and have very little to do with the big picture! The question of spending $100 billion on a high-speed train ride or between spending $20 billion building a border wall, which saves billions of dollars a year in US Homeland Security costs, drug-smuggling costs, illegal immigration enforcement costs—it seems to me so absurd that this is actually a debate. It comes down to keeping the pressure on congress to fund this wall immediately. All Trump and other Republicans need to point out is the cost of each project, more in terms of actual value or "bang for the buck": a high-speed train, which will service around eighteen million people a year, or a US-Mexico border wall. Those eighteen million riders a year estimate seems pretty high as a passenger train will only carry 1,300 passengers per train. That estimate is assuming the trains are 1,300 feet long, similar to the TGV and the AGV trains used in France and Japan. Thirty-eight train trips per day with each train filled to capacity, or 49,315 people, will have to ride the train each day, seven days a week, to hit eighteen million in ridership. Furthermore, the "California High-Speed Train Project" business plan admits that the train service will lose $700 million per year up until 2030 when all the tracks/routes are completed and ridership is up to the maximum of thirty million riders per year. Trump and his supporters need to dismiss the MSM talk that a border wall is too expensive and make sure that this task is fulfilled. A border wall that protects over three hundred million Americans each day, twenty-four hours a day is well worth the estimated cost. At the end of the day, building the border wall was also a campaign promise that Trump made at so many campaign rallies and a remark he made so often; he now owns that promise forever.

The questions that will come next for the Trump administration will be the questions of cost of the wall construction and effectiveness of the border wall or fence. The critics have said you can't build a wall or a fence over the water; well, that is not true. In Norfolk, Virginia, at the naval base, there is an underwater fence that is made of hot-tip galvanizing; these are the fences that surround the fourteen piers where naval ships are parked. These fences are constructed with modular units connected together so they can absorb water movements and levels. Flotation pontoons support the steel structure, and nets catch watercraft attempting to jump the pontoons, basically creating a floating fence. The fence can stop a very large unwanted seaworthy vessel and would certainly stop the illegal crossing of immigrants. The drug cartels are getting richer from their crimes and illegal activities, and they have more ways to smuggle people into the United States. This business of moving immigrants is still a profit center for the Mexican cartels. Building a serious wall will slow them down significantly.

CHAPTER 12

The Clinton Legacy: "Time to Stop Thinking About Tomorrow"

BILL, HILL, AND CHILL—CHILL BEING the nickname for daughter Chelsea, to go with Bill and Hill—now is the time, and the time has come to sing, "Happy Trails to You Until We Meet Again." Great classic song sung and recorded by Roy Rogers and Dale Evans. The fact is; this Roy Rogers song was most likely not a favorite of the Clinton's. Their official song was the Fleetwood Mack song, "Don't Stop Thinking About Tomorrow." Bill and Hillary seemed to love that song, and they played it everywhere and at almost every rally I ever heard or saw on television. I also saw William Jefferson Clinton alongside of Hillary for president at many of the rallies. There was a very logical reason for that to occur. Bill Clinton was a great presidential candidate, not a great president, and most definitely not a great and faithful husband. In contrast, Hillary Rodham Clinton was an awful presidential candidate in both her races against Obama in the primary elections of 2008 and later against Trump in 2016. As a campaigner she got worse, not better, as time went on. She was a disaster as the secretary of state, and history may prove she was a great danger to the national security of the United States while serving in that capacity. We can discuss the details of her use of a private, unprotected, State Department computer server later in this chapter. Chelsea Clinton, the last Clinton hope, is a nonevent and a nonstarter. She was the former vice-chairman of the Clinton Foundation, which is now a defunct operating foundation. So where do we begin and perhaps end with the Clinton legacy or Clinton dynasty?

If you are liberal or a moderate liberal, and you have earned an advanced education degree or graduate degree, you must be scratching your head and asking: How did Hillary lose the POTUS election and to Donald Trump, of all people? That is a great question; if we review the facts and history of Hillary Clinton, it is astounding that she lost. To begin Hillary went to Yale University and graduated with a degree in law; was the first lady of the state of Arkansas; first lady of the United States of America for eight years in the White House; served in the US Senate, representing the second-largest populated state in the United States, New York; served as the US secretary of state under a popular two-term president, Barack Obama; and she outspent and outraised her opponent by a significant two-to-one margin. Hillary raised and spent $1.2 billion; she broke Obama's spending record and spent the most of all time in a presidential election. Trump spent $600 million, and a big chunk was not raised; it was his own money. So how does she lose to a real-estate developer, television-show host with only a bachelor's degree, who never practiced law or even went to a law school? Even George W. Bush received an MBA from prestigious Yale University. Bush was the only US President to obtain an MBA in the history of the US presidency. Trump only graduated with the undergraduate degree; he also never served in the military and never had any experience in civil service or public office. But the most amazing fact is the Clinton POTUS campaign outspends Trump at over a two-to-one advantage. Go figure!

One reason she lost may be explained by the quote from the famous New York Yankees catcher and baseball player Yogi Berra. Yogi once said, "If you don't know where you are going, you will wind up somewhere else." I don't believe Hillary really knew where she was going or how to get there. That being said, we all know she wanted to get back to the White House, but she did not have a message to show the public good reason why she should return to the White House. Especially to return with her shady husband, coming back to have even more sexual relations in the White House and with young females working at the White House. Could it be that Hillary believed it was her God-given right to return? Had she not been very nice to all the special interests groups, LGBT, feminists, African Americans, Hispanics, teachers, the unions, and so on? Perhaps she relied on that support in those usual partnerships and alliances. But she continued to forget about a message and a goal for America. What was her message, really? Trump in contrast, had a message and a goal that could be grasped and achieved for Americans: Make America Great!

It is mind-blowing how she lost against Trump! We all have our images, thoughts, and opinions of Hillary Clinton's advantages over Donald Trump, but most of us are still perplexed. The whole answer that seems to come up over and over again is about the entire Clinton family, not just Hillary. The answer is their strange history of misdeeds, accusations of corruption, and getting caught in numerous lies actually live or recorded on television. One of Bill Clinton's big fat lies was, as he looked straight into the television camera, "I did not have sexual relations with that woman"—of course he was talking about Monica Lewinski, whom he did have sexual relations with on more than one occasion. Hillary told a big fat lie during the 2016 campaign primaries when she said, "I never had any classified information on my personal server." Who could forget this lie told by Hillary on September 11, 2012, at 10:00 p.m.—while the assault on the Benghazi, Libya, compound and attack leading to the death of Ambassador Chris Stevens was still going on, Hillary issued this statement, "Some have sought to justify the vicious behavior as a response to inflammatory material posted on the Internet." She was referring to the video *The Innocence of Muslims*, produced by, Nakoula Basseley Nakoula, who, one day after it was released on the Internet, was arrested for violating his probation here in the United States. Later on the Libyan government conceded that they were no riots in Benghazi on Sept 11 2012. The killing was, in fact, premeditated murder planned by a terrorist group. Worst of all, Hillary decided to sit still, leaving the Americans in the compound unprotected. It also turns out she denied requests for increased security in

Libya and also specifically Benghazi. On January 22, 2014, Gregory Hicks, former deputy chief of mission in Libya, stated to the *Wall Street Journal*, "Chris Stevens was not responsible for the reduction in security personnel. His requests for additional security were denied."

But history may show that the worst of the Clinton cover-ups, deceptions, and direct evil deeds may have come with the untimely death of Vincent Foster on July 20, 1993. Ultimately his death was determined a suicide by the Washington Park police, but the evidence shows quite the contrary. The park police had jurisdiction to investigate this case because Vince died in Fort Marcy Park off George Washington Parkway in Virginia. Having the park police be in charge of the initial investigation of the Vincent Foster death is like having Barney Fife from the *Andy Griffith* television show leading the investigation. Maybe the park ranger in the *Yogi Bear* cartoon television show would have been a better choice. Truth be told, Kenneth Star, the special prosecutor appointed to investigate Bill Clinton, did bring in the FBI, and they investigated, but the evidence was so bad it would have been almost impossible to really solve the case. Here are some of the botched and strange circumstances of the case. First, the Washington Park police do not have a forensics lab or forensics experts on the payroll. Perhaps that has changed, but at the time when the death occurred on one employed in this capacity. Second, the photographer for the park police took eighteen polaroid pictures; however, they were all underexposed and could not even be used. Third, four of the paramedics who arrived on the scene and who moved the body to the morgue claim there were two gunshot wounds. One wound on the side of the neck which appeared the size of a .22 caliber bullet wound and the other gunshot wound where Vince was shot through the mouth. Fourth, the Kenneth Star report never verified the side of the neck wound. The EMT who made this statement regarding the neck wound to investigators was Richard Arthur. Fifth, Richard Arthur also stated under oath that Foster's hands were lying neatly at his sides which would be highly unusual after the body is shot while seated and then he would fall in one direction, sending the arms also out in a particular direction. Sixth, the gun was still in Foster's hand, though it should normally fall out of his hand and not still be in the grasp after the shot was made. Seventh, there were no powder or muzzle flash burns in the inside of the mouth of Foster, which should have been present during the autopsy investigation. Eighth, no bullet or bullets were ever found at the scene, which translated to the conclusion that someone removed the bullets because they did not want to leave possible evidence behind. The forensic and death investigation went on for several years, with over one hundred people interviewed. There were no witnesses of the shooting, and no even claimed to have heard a gunshot. That would prove that perhaps a silencer was used. Foster's gun was fired, but no one is certain who fired it. Let it further be noted that the most significant fact is that the lead investigator US Attorney Miguel Rodriguez resigned from the US Department of Justice on January 17, 1995, because he protested the findings of Kenneth Star that the Vincent Foster death was a suicide. He wrote a letter to Kenneth Star, saying, "You have forced me to leave my job due to your decision that this death of Vincent Foster was a suicide." Perhaps it was obvious to Mr. Rodriguez that too many things just did not add up for this to be a suicide. Mr. Rodriguez to this day totally disagrees with the suicide findings.

Vince Foster was still married to his college sweetheart, with three young children. Taking one's life and leaving behind a wife and three Children is a tough pill to swallow. It was stated that Vince was suffering from "clinical depression"; the Clintons tend to have that effect on those around them. It has been well documented how "mean" Hillary was to Secret Service personnel. Many ex Secret Service agents have stated that she was difficult to be around, and often times those on the protection detail at the White House also assigned to her travel protection were berated by her.

Vincent Foster had an extremely close relationship with both Bill and Hillary Clinton. Vincent Foster was born on January 15, 1945, in the same town as Bill Clinton—Hope, Arkansas. He was a brilliant lawyer. He graduated first in his class in 1971 from University of Arkansas Law School, passed the bar with the highest recorded score ever, and worked at the Rose Law

Firm. He joined them in 1971, immediately after the successful passing of the bar examination. He also became a partner at the Rose Law Firm. Hillary and Vince Foster worked together at Rose for over ten years. Vince joined President Bill Clinton as the deputy White House counsel in 1992, just after Bill Clinton was elected. The theory was that Vince was a straight shooter. and he was bullied by both Bill and Hillary Clinton. There were many hidden past and present dealings with both the Clintons, and the "Travelgate" scandal just had emerged in the newspapers. The motive may have been for the Clintons to get rid of Vince. The speculation by many is, "Vince, you just know too much; you have to go!" The motive of either or both of the Clintons' plotting and ordering removal of Vince has never come to light, but the case for suicide does look weak and not an accurate conclusion, based on the evidence. On the contrary, the word homicide does look to be accurate. Why was the loss of Vince Foster a big deal to the Clintons? Because Vince was a lifelong friend and a key adviser. It is a mystery and most likely will never be revealed.

The Clinton Foundation has not been fully investigated, and I believe the shoe has not dropped yet. Most experts agree that the Clintons would be guilty of charity fraud using the Clinton Foundation and the Clinton Global Initiative for self–enrichment, self-dealing, and diverting charitable donations to personal account and their personal expenses. When the Clintons came up with the idea of having their own foundation, it was, by far, the smartest activity they have ever put together. It is also the largest money-making activity they have been able to financially leverage for money in their pockets. It is a great way to create self-enrichment, pay all your expenses for worldwide travel, and engage in pay-to-play or kickback activities. First you need to understand the dos and don'ts of the 501(C)3 world. Unlike all private family foundations, like the Trump Foundation, Warren Buffet Foundation, or Bill and Melinda Gates Foundation, the Clinton Foundation is not a private foundation. It was formed and operated as a "public charity." The Clinton Foundation also has been qualified as having a "worldwide mission status." Worldwide mission status means they can operate overseas and carry out a charitable purpose overseas, whereas a private foundation cannot operate overseas, Also—and no small thing—you can accept donations from foreign countries or foreign donors. The other private family foundations mentioned above are private foundations. There is a huge difference between a public charity and a private foundation in numerous ways, not to mention the worldwide mission status mentioned above. The biggest difference has to do with fund-raising. The Clinton Foundation is not restricted as a family foundation is with fund-raising. The private foundations don't get a lot of help from outside donors because they are so restricted, and most are nonoperating foundations that can only give out grants to other public charities. Public charities, in order to qualify as such, must have at least three nonfamily members as directors or as acting board members. Having said that, Bill Clinton was the president of the Clinton Foundation and Chelsea was the vice-chairman. They had other directors on the board, but they were puppets. Bill and Chelsea were the decision makers. The one point I must make is that Hillary is in the clear as far as prosecution goes. Bill and Chelsea are on the hook because they run the foundation and make the financial decisions. Hillary is not on the board and not a director. Remember when the bumper stickers said, "Hillary for Prison"? Well, the reality is she may go to a prison but just to visit. She would instead be visiting Bill and Chelsea for charity fraud.

Hillary, after her devastating loss to Trump, was very vocal on who or what was at fault for her defeat. She has, of course, blamed the Russians, James Comey, the Democratic Party, Fox News, Debbie Wasserman Schultz, John Podesta, Facebook, Twitter, religious people, the vast right-wing conspiracy. Who she has not blamed is her husband Bill and herself for having forty years' worth of baggage. Most of the baggage is highly negative and leaves a lasting legacy of dirty deeds, corruption, self-enrichment, greed, lies, and cover-ups. Trump may be, rude, crude, brash, and even unattractive, but he still does not own or even come close to the baggage the Clintons own!

CHAPTER 13

Who Will Run against Trump in 2020?

"Winning isn't everything; it is the only thing," Vince Lombardi, the famous coach of the Green Bay Packers, once said. It appears the Democrats didn't listen to Vince. They keep losing elections over and over again. In the 2018 midterm elections, they predict they will make a great comeback. The DNC claims to now have a strategy in place and a strong movement. The problem is, no one knows what the strategy is, and who is the named outright leader to get the movement going?

Chuck Schumer, Eric Holder, Jerry Brown, Elizabeth Warren, Kamala Harris, Sally Yates, Bernie Sanders, Michael Bloomberg, Michelle Obama, Oprah Winfrey—these are the names that emerge lately to take on Trump in 2020. For that matter, it could really be anyone out of the blue who emerges as the Democratic presidential candidate.

Last time around, in the 2016 election primaries, really only two Democrats ran for POTUS: Bernie and Hillary, and the third guy was a poser. Can anyone remember his name? In Las Vegas they would call this third candidate "a shill." A shill is someone who sits down at a gambling table and joins in the action with other players. He or she makes the table look more active, and if the shill is winning, that attracts more players to join in. The shills are actually playing for the house, and they use the house's money to gamble with the rest of the players. The Democratic primary race was very boring in the beginning, and their primary debates had low television audiences compared to the Republicans. Perhaps they need a few more candidates, or the DNC could have inserted a few more shills. It was clear from the DNC perspective that Hillary was going to win at all costs and that Bernie Sanders was an outsider trying to buck the system. It was also clear, using Las Vegas terms, that "it was a rigged game." Trump referred to the process as a "rigged system," but for Bernie, it actually came true. Well into the primary voting season, when Bernie started winning some key states, the television ratings increased. Now that people were watching, the Clinton corruption machine had to spring into action. The certain downfall of Bernie's chances was when the DNC decided that during the entire primary campaign, there would be only nine debates and four nationally televised debates. The republicans had twelve nationally televised debates.

The Democratic 2016 race was a stark contrast to the seventeen Republicans running for POTUS against Trump. Trump beating all seventeen was a remarkable achievement. Not only beating seasoned established politicians but at least five of them who could have given Hillary a strong battle and a run to POTUS. Jeb Bush was the strongest front runner, and he faded quickly. Ted Cruz was the favorite of many and should, if logic prevailed, have beaten Trump in the primaries. In a previous chapter, it was discussed how Trump's use of nicknames became a battle cry for Trump to repeat over and over again "Lying Ted." John Kasich, governor of Ohio should have been able to jump out in front of Trump. He has been a very popular and successful governor of a key state in the political world. Kasich just did not make it on the national stage. He looked rattled by Trump in the debates and seemed out of sorts. He appeared shocked that someone like Trump, with no political background or experience in government, could actually be a candidate for POTUS.

Who Are the Most Likely to Have a Chance against Trump in 2020?
First let us start with the most popular on the list, but this person most likely will not run for POTUS.

Oprah Winfrey—Oprah running against Trump may be the battle for the ages. In many ways she has a lot in common with Trump. She is very wealthy, she doesn't need the fame or the limelight, she has multiple homes, she travels the world, she is a very successful businesswoman, and she has been on television and starred in movies extensively. Of course their political beliefs are very different from each other, and she and Trump have a big difference in their chosen friends. Don't count on Oprah visiting or staying in the White House anytime soon under the Trump administration like she did multiple times under the Obama White House. Oprah has very liberal Hollywood friends and neighbors living up in Santa Barbara, California. She is close to Al Gore and considers him an eco-crusader. She believes and backs the thought that our planet is being devastated by climate change. The July 2017 edition of *O Magazine* promotes Al Gore's new documentary, *An inconvenient Sequel: Truth to Power*. Of course Gore's newest book is still about climate change, now the new word for global warming. Oprah has some major weak points compared to Trump, and it comes down to her support system. Oprah does not really have an immediate family like Trump. Steadman Graham is her "partner," and they are not married. She has no children. This makes it tougher to stand the rigors of a long run for political office. I am wondering who would be at her side and helping lift her spirits and confidence along the way. Her siblings seem to be close to her, but that won't help with the immediate family thing. If she won, she would be the only president to occupy the White House who was not married. Oprah was quoted as saying once, "I am not sure about the word 'wife,' and I couldn't be a wife because the word holds responsibilities I am not capable of handling."

Most political pundits doubt that Oprah will run for POTUS in 2020, but I am not so sure. She is only sixty-three years old, and she is worth $3 billion. What could be her next milestone if not POTUS? She is formidable from a public speaking standpoint and appears great on television. She could raise a ton of money. She may receive some pressure to run for POTUS from her close friends and women's advocacy groups because those groups and Democrats in general do not have an attractive or plausible candidate at this time. Altogether they may convince her that it would be the right thing to do to run for POTUS in 2020.

Michelle Obama—When all the smoke clears from her husband's legacy and his time in the oval office, the Obama legacy may be a bad memory. Michelle was a very well-respected first lady in the White House. Barack and Michelle have a nice family, and they play well as a popular family, but there are the detractors: Obamacare; Russian hacking investigations; unmasking; Susan Rice; Benghazi and the deaths of Ambassador Chris Stevens and his protection detail, Sean Smith, Tyrone Woods, and Glen Doherty; Loretta Lynch as the cover up for Hillary's e-mail server, calling it a "matter" with James Comey, ex FBI Director; the Arizona tarmac meeting between Lynch and Bill Clinton; Eric Holder and his reign as attorney general and the incredibly awful Obama decisions that are now beginning to surface regarding past policies.…Unfortunately for Michelle, these issues are still warm in the eyes of many Americans, and Michelle may want to sit this election out for 2020. Many feel it would be too soon for her to make the run for POTUS.

Michael Bloomberg is short, very short—five foot seven. He may have fared better around the 1770s when the average male in the United Kingdom or early colonial days of America was five feet two inches tall and weighed around 130 pounds. Today not so much. Bloomberg is seventy-five years old, which would make him seventy-eight and seventy-nine years old when he took office. That would make him the oldest [resident to take office in the history of all US presidents. However, Michael Bloomberg is rich, very rich—about $50.4 billion at last estimate, and according to the *Forbes* 2017, on the hundred richest in America list, he ranks number six. If he decided to fund a campaign for POTUS, he could spend more than Hillary and Trump combined in the 2016 POTUS election by at least eighteen times over.

Bloomberg is no slouch politically. He was the mayor of New York City, largest city in the United States, and he did an outstanding job in several areas: dropping crime, increasing business and commerce, and the real-estate values of the city continue to skyrocket. He is described as a businessman and by all accounts has been incredibly successful in that arena. His popularity waned somewhat as the city mayor. He started crusades against drinking soft drinks and cigarette smoking and wanted everyone to ride bicycles everywhere. He discouraged the New York cabs and even public transportation over pedal power. In 2013 he had very low approval ratings.

Joe Biden, aka Uncle Joe, is the former forty-seventh vice-president of the United States for eight years with Barack Obama. Joe Biden has been in political office longer than many of the Congress and Senate members have been alive. Joe Biden took political office on January 3,1973, and never left until January 20, 2017. That is forty-four years in a US political office. Joe Biden was born Joseph Robinette Biden Jr. on November 20, 1942, in Scranton, Pennsylvania. He is going to be seventy-five years of age on November 2017. If Joe were to run for President of the United States and if elected, he would be seventy-eight years old fifteen days after the election. If he served in office for eight years, he would eighty-six years of age and by far the oldest sitting president. Joe actually started out as a registered independent in 1968, but in 1969 Joe switched to Democrat. Growing up Joe lived in Scranton Pennsylvania for ten years before moving with his family to Delaware. His mother was Catherine Eugenia "Jean" Biden Finnegan, and his father was Joseph Robinette Biden Sr. Joe Jr. was the first of four children born into an Irish Catholic family. Joe Biden Sr. suffered some serious business setbacks, and the Biden family moved to an apartment in Claymont, Delaware. Joe Biden Sr. became somewhat successful as a used-car salesman, and the family was middle class, not wealthy or upper class. Biden attended Archmere Academy in Claymont, Delaware, where he was a standout football player and also played on the baseball team. He was elected class president during his junior and senior years. He graduated in 1961. He earned his bachelor of arts in a double major in history and political science from the University of Delaware in 1965. In 1964 while on spring break, he met Neilia Hunter, and they were married in 1966 at a Catholic church in Skaneateles, New York. Joe Moved to Syracuse, New York, to attend law school, and he received his juris doctor degree in 1968 and was admitted to the Delaware state bar in 1969. Biden never served in the armed services; he received student draft deferment during this period, and at the peak of the Vietnam War, in 1968, he was reclassified by the Selective Service System as not available for service due to having had asthma as a teenager. Biden actually started in politics in 1969 when he ran as a Democrat for the New Castle County Council in Delaware on a liberal platform; that platform included Biden supporting public housing. He won by a solid margin. In 1972 Biden announced he was running for US senator from the state of Delaware. In 1972 the Republican Senator, J. Caleb Boggs, appeared unbeatable, and no other Democrat wanted to go against him. Biden's campaign had no money and virtually given no chance of winning. Biden's sister was his campaign manager. During the summer of the campaign, he was trailing by thirty points. His energy level, his attractive family, and a good ability to connect with voters gave him optimism. This also gave the surging Biden an advantage over the older and ready-to-retire Boggs. Biden won in November 7, 1972, in an upset of a 3,162 vote margin. Tragedy struck just a few weeks after the election; Biden's wife and one-year-old daughter were killed in an automobile accident while Christmas shopping in Hockessin, Delaware. They were hit by a tractor trailer while she pulled out from the intersection. The truck driver was cleared of all wrongdoing. Biden's two sons were also in the car but survived the accident with no long-term effects.

At age thirty, the minimum age required to hold the office of senator, Biden became the sixth-youngest US Senator in history. Biden ran for the Democratic presidential nomination in 1988; he was attempting to become the youngest president since John F. Kennedy. Biden's campaign began to lose steam when he was questioned about using words from other speeches in his own speeches—in other words, he was plagiarizing. Then a video was released showing that he bragged that he graduated in the top half of his law school class and had attended law school on a full scholarship; these claims turned out to be untrue or gross exaggerations of his actual record. Biden ran again for president in 2008; he rapidly fell behind to Hillary Clinton and Barack

Obama in the primaries. Biden dropped out early because he also had trouble raising the money necessary to mount a serious campaign. He never got above single digits in the national polls. Biden was still reelected to the US Senate six additional terms, in 1978, 1984, 1990, 1996, 2002, and 2008. On August 22, 2008, Obama announced that he was selecting Biden to be his running mate as vice-president just after he won the nomination for POTUS. Joe is very much a long shot to run again for POTUS in 2020. He has never worked in the private sector, only as a lawyer, and his lack of experience in business would also make him a target. Voters would surmise he has been a career politician his entire life.

Now let's look at those candidates who are more likely to run against Trump:

Elizabeth Warren, aka Pocahontas: Before we have a discussion of Elisabeth Warren, it is important to know who Pocahontas is and why she had an important role in history. In December 1607, while seeking food along the Chickahominy River in Virginia, Captain John Smith, the famous English explorer and settler of the Jamestown Colony in Virginia, was captured by the Powhatan Indians.

Captain Smith was the leader of the Jamestown colony, the first permanent colony to be established as an English colony in the United States. John Smith was born in England in January 1580, and at age sixteen, he quickly took to the sea. John Smith was a man of the oceans and a land explorer, soldier, and author. He was the first English explorer to map the Chesapeake Bay area and New England.

The Pocahontas encounter with John Smith and the courage of this woman was demonstrated during the capture. The Chief who also the Father of Pocahontas began the execution of John Smith by striking the head of Smith with his war club. The story goes that Pocahontas draped herself over the body of John Smith and placed her head over his head as the blow was delivered.

She took the blow instead and saved his life, according to the story told by John Smith. Many historians doubted this event, but nevertheless, they both lived. If the story is true, then this is an amazing case of courage and strength carried out by a native American woman.

Now we fast forward to Elizabeth Warren. She is no Pocahontas. Not even close. Her maiden name is Herring, and she was born in June 22, 1949, in Oklahoma City, Oklahoma. There is no family history where she is related to Native American Indians. She spent time in Houston, Texas, where she got her BS degree in speech pathology and audiology from the University of Houston. She married Jim Warren, and she and her husband moved to New Jersey for his work. There she went to law school and received her JD degree from Rutgers University in 1976. She and Jim Warren divorced in 1978, and she did remarry but kept her name from the first husband, Warren. Most of her career has been teaching at law schools throughout the country and not in the actual legal practice arena.

She won the Massachusetts US Senate election in 2012, the first time she has ever run for political office. She defeated Scott Brown, a Republican. She got the name Pocahontas after her opponent Scott Brown discovered that while she tenured in the mid-1990s at Harvard law school, Warren described herself as a minority in the law school directory and touted herself as a Native American faculty member. She has also used language describing herself as having Cherokee and Delaware Indian ancestry. She gave a direct quote to the CNN television show *Starting Point*: "I'm proud of my Native American Heritage." The *New England Historical Genealogical Society* quotes, "Our society has no proof of her Cherokee dissent." She has been dishonest about the whole thing and therefore an insult to the name "Pocahontas."

Many political experts believe she will run for POTUS in 2020; again she will be older than the DNC prefers at age seventy-one but still younger than Bernie, Hillary or Biden.

Kamala Harris is now the newest senator from California. She has strong political and legal background, which qualifies her to run for POTUS, and also some attractive reasons to be a Democratic candidate. She is young at age fifty-two, and she is attractive and will appear well on television. She was recently married to Douglas Emhoff in 2014. Douglas is a very successful corporate attorney based in Los Angeles. Emhoff rubs elbows with a lot of the power brokers in business and entertainment world. Kamala is also listed as African American and Native American, so she has the triple-plus background going for her. It includes her standing with two minority groups, and she is a woman. She became California attorney general in 2011 and was reelected. Prior to that, she was San Francisco's district attorney from 2004 to 2011. She is an average public speaker, and with some coaching, she could be a formidable candidate and debater. It will all depend on if the Democrats think she has enough popularity and name recognition. They—the Democrats—may be seeking a bigger name and a bigger voice and someone who has had a significant amount of national exposure.

Bernie Sanders is still the acting US senator from the state of Vermont. He continues to have a strong voice in the Senate despite his campaign loss to Hillary in November. Bernie won twenty-three state primary contests and amassed thirteen million votes. He was really close to taking down the Clinton machine. "Feel the Bern" was the battle cry for the Bernie voters. The timing for another POTUS run for Bernie is not the best. The voters of America are getting older, and the older set are not as fond of a socialist agenda. The elderly are suspicious of free government programs like free college tuition, which Bernie has promised if he is elected. The biggest determent to Bernie would be his age he would be seventy-nine years old at election time. This would make him the oldest president to run for office and the oldest president to occupy the office of POTUS. Bernie plays well with the liberals because he is basically a socialist. This has been Bernie's strength with the younger set—those voters with high student debt, looking for free college tuition and basically a laundry list of free stuff from the federal government. Bernie is so out of touch that he scares the Democratic Party, and I doubt they wish to take a chance on his run for POTUS. The Democrats do not want to get crushed again in a national race, and it will be difficult for the Dems to win back the Senate or Congress if their Senate and House candidates have to get behind a socialist like Bernie. The fate of Bernie for "one more time" does not look good and his age is working against him.

Eric Holder is perhaps the most outspoken of the current Trump resistance movement. Mr. Holder has recently moved to California to get in bed with powerful Democrats and powerful political elected officials like Governor Jerry Brown, Gavin Newsome, Kamala Harris, Diane Feinstein, and others. Holder has been quoted as saying, "States have rights to resist the federal government and resist oppression from the federal government." Holder has an extensive background in the legal system and politics. He was one of the longest-serving attorney generals under President Obama. He served from 2009 until 2015. He announced he would be stepping down in late 2014, and on September 30, 2014, his approval rating had fallen to 26 percent. The only notable person in the federal government who had a lower rating was Eric Shinski at 18 percent. She was the former Health and Human Services director in charge when the VA facilities falsified records to cover up the long wait times at the VA hospitals. Holder is also a New Yorker from Bronx, New York. He also attended Columbia University for his undergraduate degree and his J.D. degree from Columbia Law school. Eric Holder is popular among many liberal Democrats and knows powerful people. I would question perhaps his ability to connect with Americans when it comes to running for office. He does have baggage with a "fast and furious gun-running campaign with the DEA agents," and he did very little on the war on drugs and drug smuggling. He would be a long shot to get the nomination if he decides to run for POTUS.

Sally Yates was born on August 20, 1960, in Atlanta, Georgia. Her father was an attorney and a judge from Georgia. Sally graduated from the University of Georgia with a bachelor of arts degree in journalism in 1982 and a juris doctor degree in 1986, also from the University of Georgia. In so many words, Sally has emerged as the new daring and hero of the Democratic party. When she resisted the executive order Trump travel ban on six Muslim countries, Trump fired her for not backing a direct decision and a direct executive order. I don't think most people who work in the private sector with their bosses believe that this was unfair. In the private sector, if you ignore or oppose a direct order from your boss, you're going to be terminated. She was praised by Chuck Schumer and Nancy Pelosi for opposing Trump and the travel ban. Mrs. Yates was the acting US Attorney General for ten days during the Trump administration, from January 20, 2017, to January 30, 2017. Trump was in the process of appointing Jeff Sessions, but Mr. Sessions had not been approved by the Senate confirmation hearings as yet. Sally Yates has a distinguished career in government service and in the legal profession. She is my "long shot" choice for the Democratic party presidential nominee in 2020, but she has not been in the limelight very long. But neither had Obama been in the limelight for a long period of time.

Chuck Schumer is the current US Senate minority leader. Charles Ellis Schumer was born in 1950 in Brooklyn, New York—another New Yorker like Trump. He still lives in Brooklyn today. He is a longtime political figure, and he represents the second largest US state, population-wise: the state of New York. He may be close to having one of the longest records continuously serving as a politician. He has been in politics since 1975 as a US senator. He has been in politics for forty-two years, all to elected offices. He served in the New York Senate from 1975 until 1980 and then ran for US Congress, where he served from 1981 until 1999. He was elected to the US Senate with an outstanding educational background, graduating from Harvard undergraduate school and then from Harvard law school in 1975. He actually received a perfect score of 1,600 on his college SATs. With all the education and experience in politics, I guess the Democrats have chosen or anointed Schumer to be the most outspoken within his own party and to the speak to the media regarding the Trump presidency and administration. Schumer never avoids an opportunity for television interviews, especially if those interviews can include an opportunity to criticize Trump and his administration. Schumer will continue to attack Trump, and if he is successful in bringing Trump down, then he would be the front runner for the Democratic presidential nomination in 2020. Schumer will keep pounding away at Trump, and from the support he gets from the Democrats, it is his best path to the White House in 2020. He does annoy a lot of people, and look for Trump to keep up the "Cryin' Chuck" nickname. If Chuck does take on Trump in the 2020 debates, look for Trump to win those debates handily.

CHAPTER 14

What or Who Can Bring down Trump While Still in Office?

THE "DEEP STATE": WHAT EXACTLY is the "deep state"? Some people claim it is a large group, in power positions, well-funded and highly organized to remove Donald Trump from office by any means necessary. Names like George Soros have been linked to heavy funding of the "resistance movement" and the demonstrations organized across the United States and even overseas. Someone has to pay those protestors to show up, right? How else do these groups have the money for transportation, food, signs, staging areas and logistical gatherings? The Women's March the day after the 2016 presidential inauguration of Trump was highly organized and planned. The buses arrived in downtown Washington, DC by the thousands. I was there personally, and I witnessed it all firsthand, live and in living color. Taking the conspiracy theories out of the "deep state" equation, we really get down to the underbelly of what is the actual "deep state." It is a combination of fake or false information being leaked to the press, corruption, dirty politics, payoffs, paid activists, and government insiders as the Obama holdovers who won't give up the Obama legacy of "Hope and Change." I suspect the deep state is not as deep as believed. The real deep state are the leakers who don't regard the consequences—the Obama and Clinton advocates who want to prove that Trump is not legit and needs to be harassed, embarrassed, and revealed for his mistakes and even his selections of his staff members and White House staff. There is evidence that a deep state does also exist within the Republican Party also. There are the "never Trump" people who are turncoats within the party. The reason they are turncoats is that they are engaged in the cronyism and the system of insider corruption. Finally, after 124 leaks in 125 days of the Trump presidency, someone is fighting back on behalf of the Trump White House. US Attorney General Jeff Sessions announced new efforts to find and prosecute those who leak private conversations and classified information to the press. Sessions announced that the FBI would be stepping up its efforts. The number of Justice Department leak investigators would triple in the near future. The Obama administration took an aggressive stance against finding leakers but never prosecuted any journalists in the entire time he was in office. In 2015 Eric Holder Jr., the then-US attorney general, announced that some of the Justice Department's investigations aimed at reporters had gone too far. He actually changed policy to make it more difficult for prosecutors to go after journalists' records. At this time, there is no report or evidence that Sessions has taken on any of Eric Holder's policies or if they have been reversed.

With the deep state, you have individuals creating a power base, and having that base maintained is more important than principles, morals, and doing what is right. The leaders and the followers of the deep state have lost the more important principals of serving in the US government and serving the people of the United States.

Scandals and hidden secrets: The media has tried on this one, and they keep trying to get any kind of dirt on President Trump and his family. Make no mistake, the MSM will keep searching for the dirty secrets that can harm Trump. The Billy Bush Access Hollywood hidden audio was really a dangerous time for "The Donald" and no laughing matter. The dialogue in the bus with Billy Bush was so dramatic to many women, and I believe many won't ever get over it. Trump's career in the private sector and in the television world with many beautiful women around as "eye candy"—most of us could see how this could happen. Powerful businessmen, talent agents, and celebrities are going to have encounters with attractive women who really expect the be the subject of sexist remarks. Not a shocker in the world of television and the entertainment industry. Scandals also sell newspapers and get people to watch television. At some point it becomes just too much, and I think most Americans are reaching that point with the media.

Health issues: Not likely that Trump drops dead from a heart attack or a stroke. Trump may brag about many things he has accomplished, but his claim that he is very healthy has been medically verified. His personal habits are not detriments to health. He does not smoke, unlike Barack Obama, who entered the White House as a chain smoker; he does not drink alcohol; and he exercises and plays golf, which seems to be an activity that prolongs life based on the history of long lives of professional golfers. The presidency seems to be a grind but many, in fact most, US presidents are living extra-long lives—much longer than the general population. Mortality tables for men in the United States are still below eighty years of age. Gerald Ford was in his nineties before he died; Jimmy Carter is ninety-two years old; and George H. W. Bush is ninety-three years old, born June 12, 1924. Ronald Regan lived to be ninety-four, born in 1911.

Assassination: The last president killed while still in office was John F. Kennedy and he was supposedly shot by an ex–US Marine. Lee Harvey Oswald, the purported assassin, was the accused, and there is no question Oswald fired the rifle aimed at Kennedy from the Dallas book depository. After that clear fact, it becomes very questionable who really shot Kennedy in the head. Doubt has been cast by several forensics experts that Oswald was the true assassin. It does not prove logical that Oswald got the "kill shot" on President Kennedy. The most obvious question was, how could the piece from the back of Kennedy's head project and actually go backward, landing on the back hood of the moving automobile? How could that be possible when in fact Oswald was behind Kennedy? Simple physics tells us the piece of the skull and the brain matter should have shot forward and not in a backward trajectory. Mrs. Kennedy was seen in the McGruder video grabbing the human brain matter and piece of her husband's skull.

Abraham Lincoln was shot by an actor at close range. Don't count on that occurring anytime soon. I don't think anyone will get that close to this president, and I am pretty sure it won't be an actor who makes another kill shot at point-blank range. When Lincoln was shot, it was the same day the Secret Service was formed. The Secret Service was established for protection detail only after the death of President Lincoln. The Secret Service was formed on July 5, 1865. And it was formed not to protect the president; it was formed under the Treasury department to prevent the illegal production or counterfeiting of money. This modern Secret Service is too well trained and prepared for any and all kinds of attacks and assassination attempts. Those who could possibly be successful would have to be highly trained ex-military from the US special forces or another country who can deliver a bomb, drone strike, or military ordinance. It is unlikely a pure terrorist group could get to POTUS. It is never a good idea to get complacent when it comes to presidential protection detail, however, and if Trump follows the rules of the protection detail, he should be fine.

Declaration of war and/or major attack on the United States: This would cause a situation that either defines a president or gives that same president a major setback due to the blame of the situation. Today that threat could actually happen in a number of hot spots around the world, but none of them more dangerous than North Korea. Americans are tired of helping other countries who are on the brink of war or are engaged in a civil war or a border war with a rival country over territory disputes. Those countries either don't appreciate what we do for them or turn on us and accuse the United State of making a bad situation worse off. I must say, in the past twenty-five years, the latter has been the case. We have not created a good situation for the Middle East. It was our goal to stop the fighting over there, and we failed at the task. North Korea is a whole other story. The North Koreans have selected the United States as their main enemy. The reason they single us out is that we are the richest country in the world, and we have the most effective military. They also believe we will be the first to back down and not pick a fight with them. If they can hold out for a few more years, they will have enough military might to most extort the United States.

The economy: It is no joke that a good or bad economy affects elections and the attitudes of voters. After President George W. Bush, the American people blamed the Republicans for the awful economy, including the credit crisis, mortgage meltdowns, loss of real-estate home values, and high unemployment. John McCain, although he was too boring and set in his thinking to beat the upstart Obama at the ballot box, did not really stand a chance because he was a Republican also getting blamed for the awful economy. The newer generation may be less greedy and self-serving than in past generations. There are some trends showing that they are content with having less money and even fewer things than past generations. The Bible says in 1 Timothy 6:10 that "the love of money is a root of all evil." I wonder if Bill Gates believes that? Now compare the average life in the United States with the super-rich like Bill Gates. In reality most Americans have it the same way as Bill Gates. Both the average American and Bill Gates both get a hot shower in the morning; we sleep on clean sheets in a heated or air-conditioned house; we own multiple television sets, smartphones, computers, cars, and trucks; we wake up to hot coffee and fresh orange juice; we go out to movies and play golf, tennis, softball, or bowling; go swimming in the ocean, pool, or lake; and take vacations. Bill has a bigger house than us; when we fly, we get one seat on the plane, whereas he owns the whole jet; when he goes on vacation, he takes a private yacht that he owns; but all in all, the differences are not that great.

One more thing to add: most billionaires and multimillionaires are not always the happiest people. Here are some quotes from famous wealthy individuals:

"I have made many millions, but they have brought me no happiness."
—John D. Rockefeller

"I was happier when I was doing a mechanic's job." —Henry Ford

"The care of $200,000,000 is enough to kill anyone, there is no pleasure in it." —W. H. Vanderbilt

"Millionaires seldom smile." —Andrew Carnegie

Money Can't Buy Me Love," written and recorded by the Beatles, 1964

A couple of words of wisdom about money:

- Money can buy a book but not wisdom
- Money can buy a watch but not time
- Money can buy blood but not a life
- Money can buy a toy but not joy
- Money can buy a bed but not sleep
- Money can buy a position but not respect
- Money can buy a house but not a home

Trump has the wind at his back right now because the US economic situation is very strong and has improved with his policies and his rollback on regulations. The US stock market is at all-time highs, real estate values going up or holding steady, employment up, and it is well documented that during his first six months in office, hundreds of thousands of new jobs became available or were created by businesses and not by the growth of the federal, state, or local governments.

The Mainstream press: A lot of what is going on with the MSM was discussed in previous chapters. If the press can't take Trump down with authentic news reporting, then they will try to take him down with false reporting and inventing stories. The left has gone wild about finding something that would stick. It would be really a farce and tragic on the American public to have any president impeached, indicted, or forced to resign about a false series of accusations that have absolutely no evidence. Watergate was the first and only example where a newspaper and the reporters were so effective with their stories that they caused a sitting president of the United States to resign while still in office. But Watergate was Watergate and a much different series of events and crimes. Much different than the false news of today. Watergate not only had real evidence, they had in their custody the culprits who carried out the break-in. They were caught red-handed by the building security and the DC police. Watergate was also unique because it had a true inside leaker; he was called "Deep Throat." Deep Throat's real name was Mark Felt. Mark Felt was a career FBI agent who was second in command at FBI headquarters under J. Edgar Hoover.

The whole chain of evidence and names of who was involved in the Watergate break-in and the resulting cover up by Nixon administration personnel was supplied to two *Washington Post* reporters by Mark Felt. Those reporters whom he informed were Bob Woodward and Carl Bernstein. The very detailed information that Felt gave to Woodward and Bernstein was not classified information at the time because the FBI was not investigating the break-in. What was never revealed to the public was why the FBI would help with this story and why the FBI wished to bring down Nixon. The FBI insiders know the reason. The reason was to teach Richard Nixon a lesson. Woodward and Bernstein pressed on and discovered the facts about Watergate only through Assistant Director Mark Felt. In reality the accounts and stories of their exhaustive reporting and numerous interviews are highly embellished. It was never proven that Nixon knew about the planning of the break-in. But evidence was strong that he covered it up. Anyway, G. Gordon Liddy, working for the Nixon White House, was in charge of the break-in at the Watergate hotel and the George McGovern for President headquarters. Liddy did not order the break-in; he was the onsite organizer and executed the caper while onsite with the other Watergate burglars. Liddy did recruit his accomplices also; they were ex-Cuban agents who were opposed to Fidel Castro. Liddy, ironically, was a former FBI agent, and he was stationed in a New York office. Anyway, he resigned from the FBI to run for US Congress in upstate New York. Liddy lost in his bid to get elected, but because he also supported the Nixon POTUS campaign, he was offered a job in the Nixon administration.

Another unknown fact was that the Watergate break-in was actually justified in a legal sense because there was hard evidence that the McGovern for President campaign was in part funded by foreign enemies of the United States. Back then a legal wiretap could be ordered if it was foreign espionage involvement. McGovern was actually getting campaign money from Soviet Union backed groups. Weathermen Underground, Students for a Democratic Society, and the American Communist Workers Party. Here is where it gets very interesting, I mention in the paragraph above that Liddy did not order the Watergate break-in. It was ordered by another Nixon surrogate, Jeb Stuart Magruder, former White House aide. But unknown to everyone except the FBI and a few White House insiders was that the Liddy team was really a default team and the second choice to carry out the original break-in. The first choice for the originally planned break-in was intended as a "wiretap job." Magruder took it upon himself to call the best wiretappers at the time, namely the FBI. In fact, the name of the unit that does the "big boy" wiretaps is the "Physical Security Unit," located in the basement of the FBI headquarters building on Pennsylvania Avenue Northwest, Washington, DC. Back in the early 1970s, one of the most experienced and talented members of that unit was alone in the facility, preparing for other wiretaps, when he received a call from Jeb Magruder. The name of the special agent who took the call was Edward Tickle. Magruder gave Tickle information over the phone and said he would arrange a follow up meeting with additional instructions to come at a later date. Ed immediately went to discuss the conversation with the unit chief in charge. The unit chief told Ed he must ask the permission and approval from the FBI section chief. The section chief then reported to the assistant director of the FBI, who at the time was Mark Felt, aka Deep Throat. Assistant Director Felt then gave a report regarding the White House break-in request to Director J. Edgar Hoover. From scuttlebutt going around the bureau circles, Hoover was quite upset and angry that some aide from the White House would make this request, and he was insulted that he was not contacted directly. That was the "huge" mistake the Nixon surrogates made that day. Anyway Trump ordered Mark Felt and everyone else who has a conversation with the White House to deny the request of the break-in and wiretapping. He also told Felt, "I want you to leak this crap to Washington Post and find a few low level reporters who will write a story, and we will teach the White House a lesson this time." The moral of that story is, you do not mess with J. Edgar Hoover.

Trump has yet to appoint a replacement FBI director for the fired James Comey. Anyway, if he could get someone even close to abilities of J. Edgar Hoover, he would be in luck. I don't think he will find a Hoover type. They just don't make them like Hoover anymore!

Impeachment: It is difficult to get an actual impeachment unless there are high crimes and misdemeanors. The left has a movement, and some were demanding his impeachment even before he took office. Trump is being accused of things that did not happen but rather are things the MSM and the Democrats wish had happened. The Dems wish that Trump actually met with members of the Russian leadership and plotted together how to steal the election from Hillary Clinton. The MSM will not stop with the Trump attacks until they find their Watergate! And I predict the majority of the MSM has passed the point of no return in a search to remove Trump from office. In the end, something has to give! They are on a dangerous, misguided mission. The MSM mission is to change the world, but first they believe they must change the direction of the United States. Either the television and newsprint press will be forever ignored by America during this time frame, and in the final outcome totally separate from the Americans who now stand up for America First. If they don't get behind this agenda and do not get behind the "Trump Train," they will discover they may destroy themselves with an obsessive agenda that only thinks in one direction. We could be seeing the end of the road for the mainstream media and the fall of the Democrats, especially if they develop a kangaroo court for Trump. If they falsely accuse Trump and try to impeach him without any proof, you will see people rise up in a big way, and there will be tremendous clashes. This will turn our society upside down. Maybe this is someone's master plan to see a possible civil war in the United States. The battle lines have been drawn; it will be the conservative, hardworking middle class against the liberals and special interest groups. The left wing only knows one direction, and that direction is, "Always turn left, because there is no right!"

The RINOs: Who are the RINOs? They are Republicans dressed up and acting like conservative Republicans, but they are really lined up against Trump and his methods of running the United States of America. Another description is that they are also Republicans who say things to stay popular with the mainstream media. The RINOs are not used to seeing or having someone like Trump in charge as POTUS. The RINOs prefer an establishment representative or leader who will play the politics game to their benefit and to their liking. According to Wikipedia, the web based on line dictionary, a RINO is an acronym for "Republicans in Name Only." This type of label dates back to 1912, coming from President Teddy Roosevelt when he said there are Republicans not acting like Republicans. The actual use of the term was used by a reporter named John DiStaso working for the Manchester, New Hampshire, *Union Leader* newspaper. He used the term RINO back on December 31, 1992. We can argue the point and argue the behavior of the most active RINOS or of the least active RINOS; nevertheless, it is a travesty that Republicans place their own greed and power over supporting each other and their voters. RINOs make America weaker and not stronger. Hillary Clinton did have it right to her Democrat comrades when she put together her POTUS slogan, "Stronger Together," The Democrats do stick together on their major issues, and the Republicans do not. The case in point is that the Republicans told the American people and the media for seven years, "Just give us the US presidency, and we will get rid of Obamacare." Now that they have the majority in the US House of Representatives, the US Senate, and the POTUS, they can't stick together and pass anything that helps the American public. In some recent Republican primaries, voters have been rejecting establishment RINOs in favor of those with stronger conservative values. The biggest RINOs are the ones who promote themselves rather than the wishes or needs of the voters who elected them. Below is a list of the 2017 line up of RINOs. This list was compiled by the organization called Conservative

Review, and each name listed was rated according to the person's behavior to act as a RINO. The Conservative Review editors put together a point rating system that gives weight to the most RINO activity per listed member. The top twenty-five RINOs are listed in order, 1 through 25. Number 1 means the individual is a "huge" RINO, and position 25 would be a more toned-down RINO:

1. Paul Ryan: Speaker of the US House of Congress and a current U. S. Congressman from Iowa. His SUPER RINO rank is #1 because he does not stand up against the Democrats and back Republicans. His staff instead, researches which news stories the MSM are reporting and the opinion polls to make sure he will agree or disagree with the popular thoughts and views. He is not a risk taker, and he will stick with the establishment every time. He is possibly most dangerous because he does not project his hidden agenda or what he is doing behind the scenes with Democrats. He is in a position of strength and leadership, but he will not go down as a great leader in the Republican party; instead, he will leave a legacy of weak, ineffective leadership.
2. John McCain: US Senator from Arizona and war hero. Trump called McCain not exactly a war hero because he was captured by the Vietnamese and held captive for six years. Accounts from other soldiers stated that John McCain was tortured while in captivity, but there is no documented proof of that. Also there is no proof as to whether he held out the information from the enemy about his missions. Anyone who survives enemy captivity needs to be well respected, especially if that captivity was caused by them doing their duty to serve their own country. In that regard I give him the badge of courage as a patriot. As a politician and putting America first, I give him the lowest rank possible and ranked #2 RINO because his decisions and his voting record are killing freedom in America. He undermines Trump at every opportunity he gets, but more importantly, he is not putting us as a nation first and on top of other countries. Because of McCain the United States Congress or Senate has had zero major

legislative achievements. Nothing to show regarding tax reform, repeal and replace Obamacare, and no changes on the budget. McCain sides with liberals in many cases and reaches across the aisle to the liberal Democrats on many issues that are not conservative. He called the Tea Party people "Hobbits." He is a SUPER RINO—on July 28, he placed the final nail in the coffin of the repeal and replace Obamacare. The vote was 51 to 49 to repeal. McCain could have made the difference to repeal. He was coming off a terrible brain cancer diagnosis, which we would not wish on anyone. He went back to Washington after a few days, and the fellow Republicans claimed he was rushing back to town to save the repeal and replace vote; instead, he flip-flopped over to the Democrats' side and voted against the repeal. In the past he refused to go after Barack Obama and his administration's role in "Fast and Furious," the DEA drug- and gun-smuggling operation instigated by Eric Holder, United States attorney general serving under Barack Obama. He was opposed to both the Reagan and Bush tax cuts. He supported gay rights, abortion, and earmarks. He was in support of TPP, the Trans Pacific Partnership trade agreement, but most of all, as a RINO, he did nothing to protect our borders from illegal crossings from Mexico. He lives in a border state, Arizona, with a huge number of illegal crossings every day arriving from Mexico, and he did nothing to stop it or even slow it down. He proposed zero laws to slow down the illegal flow of immigrants into the United States. Recently President Trump banned transgenders from serving in the military. The main reason for the ban is the medical procedures were just too expensive and also cause loss of duty availability because of the long recovery time on the surgery, not to mention the monthly costs for hormone therapy. McCain has publicly protested the transgender ban and gave the following quote: "Any American who meets current medical and readiness standards should be allowed to continue serving." McCain has been elected to office in Washington, DC, for over thirty years. It is now time for him to go; unfortunately, he is not up for reelection until 2022.

3. Lisa Murkowski: US senator from Alaska who has served since 2002. Lisa is a SUPER RINO; she also voted against the vote to repeal and replace Obamacare on July 28, 2017. She was called out recently by Freedom Works and Club for Growth and for America, both conservative organizations, for betraying their promise to the American people to repeal Obamacare. On June 16, Murkowski committed to preserving in a new health-care bill and funding Planned Parenthood. Alaska is a pretty big welfare state, so perhaps that is where she is coming from, and the individual states are going to have to shell out more dollars for their in-state Medicaid costs.
4. Lindsey Graham: US senator from South Carolina who has served in Washington fourteen years. Lindsey is a SUPER RINO because since the time Trump announced his presidency, Graham has been very opposed to Trump. When Lindsey Graham also announced that he was running for president, he began his campaign insulting Donald Trump. Graham did not stand on the debate stage very long. Graham was forced to drop out early because polls showed he lacked popularity and was way too far down on the list of candidates for POTUS. When Trump started gaining momentum and became the front-runner, Graham became a very vocal critic of Donald Trump. After Trump won the POTUS election, Graham also frequently made negative comments about Trump. Here are just a few quotes from our pal Lindsey: "Trump Is empowering Vladimir Putin." "Half of what Trump does is not OK." "If you trying to connect with the people, you should not be rude, crude, and a bull in a china shop." These are a few quotes and, frankly, the most docile quotes. Graham has been undermining Trump with the media out in the open and behind closed doors with Republican leaders and Democratic leaders. He deserves a solid #4 or even a #2 rating because he schemes with Paul Ryan and John McCain in the back rooms. Lindsey is an establishment Republican, so he is afraid of someone like Trump shaking things up. Trump is putting the executive branch of the US government back in place where a lot of the "pork barrel" government programs are being

eliminated. Graham is someone who wants those programs on place because it helps him get reelected. Every time Senator Graham gets money for his state of South Carolina, he builds his power base.

5. Susan Collins: US senator from the State of Maine. She is a SUPER RINO because she voted against her own party on the repeal and replace Obamacare on July 28, 2017. She clearly does not back her fellow Republicans. It is difficult to understand her logic. Is she just incompetent, or does she have a hidden agenda like her fellow SUPER RINOs?

6. Jeff Flake: US Republican senator from Arizona has been a SUPER RINO lately, and his popularity is getting dangerously low in his home state. Flake is a becoming a huge Trump basher, and this is getting him huge kudos from the left and the Democratic party. The only problem for Flake is that his popularity is going down, according to the Democratic Firm Public Policy Polling. The latest poll shows that only 18 percent of Arizona voters approve of his performance. Just 31 percent surveyed said they would vote for Flake, and this was compared to 47 percent saying they would vote for a generic Democratic candidate. Flake is up for reelection in 2018. Flake's problem is he released a new book, *Conscience of a Conservative*, which has been referred to as a Trump hit-piece. David Brooks, who is with the *New York Times*, explains what the book is all about in his review: "A thoughtful defense of traditional conservatism and a thorough assault on the way Donald Trump is betraying it." Flake may be hiding a strategy the Republicans don't know about, but at this point, he is in jeopardy. He will have a Republican challenger in the 2018 primary elections. His challenger is Kelly Ward, who lost against John McCain, but this time it will different against Flake. The biggest difference between Ward and Flake is that Kelly Ward is a fervent Trump supporter, and Trump will be out in force supporting her.

There are Super RINOs and there are regular RINOs. The actions for a regular RINO differ from the super RINO. The SUPER RINOS are those who are hurting America and need to be removed from their office. The SUPER RINOS have shown time and again that they do not vote to help their community; they vote to promote their own agenda and their power base with the Democrats. In the case of John McCain, he can run but he can't hide from the facts. He has voted against the repeal of Obamacare—that is now public record—yet even with his own in his home State of Arizona, they have had their medical insurance premiums increased to 140 percent in 2017 in just one year. Their premiums will be rising again in 2018 to another 60 percent. McCain, unbelievable as it sounds, has opposed the Trump border wall and has done nothing about slowing down illegal immigration crossings into Arizona. I give a regular RINO more of the benefit of the doubt. Perhaps they should not be as harshly judged; some RINOs should be given a chance because they have not fallen over the cliff like the SUPER RINOs. The regular RINOS can still be effective and help this country get on the right track. They need to exercise courage, real leadership, and also back Donald Trump's agenda. These RINOs and SUPER RINOs should give up their salaries over the past seven years. People are suffering "Big League" because of Obamacare; those are the facts. The RINOs did nothing to help. How could they be so unprepared after Trump got elected to not be ready and have a "pristine plan" on health care ready to go? It almost seems like a plot to let all of America down!

Below is the list of regular RINOs:

7. Thad Cochran, RINO
8. Mitch McConnell, RINO
9. Orrin Hatch, RINO
10. Kevin McCarthy, RINO
11. Lamar Alexander, RINO
12. Bob Corker, RINO
13. Tom Cole, RINO
14. Jeff Flake, RINO
15. John Cornyn, RINO
16. Peter King, RINO

17. Mike Simpson, RINO
18. Harold Rogers, RINO
19. Don Young, RINO
20. Rob Portman, RINO
21. Cathy McMorris Rogers, RINO
22. Johnny Isakson, RINO
23. Richard Burr, RINO
24. Charlie Dent, RINO
25. Susan Brooks, RINO
26. Shelly Capito, RINO

The threat from within may not actually be who or what we know but what we have forgotten. The founders led our country to establish a republic. Representatives stood between the people and the state of the union of states. Electors, not the people or regular voters, selected the president. Senators were not originally elected by popular vote, either. Senators were elected by the state legislatures. For this new republic to succeed, voters had to be informed and responsible in choosing these representatives, and the representatives had to invoke wise counsel in order to rise above the immediate demands of the people. The core of our system of government is actually informed, involved, and responsible voters to take place in the process. The founders did have a fear of pure democracy in which the citizens would take over the laws of the nation without participation of the elected office holders. President John Adams, thirteen years after he was out of office, wrote a letter in 1814. Adams wrote the following: "Remember, democracy never lasts long. It soon wastes, exhausts, and murders itself. There never was a democracy yet that did not commit suicide. When clear prospects are opened before vanity, pride, avarice, or ambition, for their easy gratification, it is hard for the most considerate philosophers and the most conscientious moralists to resist the temptation. Individuals have conquered themselves. Nations and large bodies of men, never." The Constitution needed to rise above the passions or wants of the people. The individual is sovereign, not the rulers, yet the rulers must make sure that these things are rational from the people. Willful refusal to seek the good of the nation on the most important issues is a necessity. For the whole democratic system to work, the voters have to be informed and not misled. When I say informed, I mean they have to be proactive and do their own research. Today the spin and the media is relentless. Candidates are peppered with nonsense questions and questions that are absolutely designed to get someone off track. We will lose our democracy if our policy is dictated by just public opinion polls, and even worse would be if the policy of the land now becomes laws of the land based on campaign contributions alone. Accepting large contribution checks will encourage corruption. It is now the basis of democracy to resist the wants of the few because it will benefit their desires over the wants and needs of nation. Trump is not perfect, but he did not play the favorites game with anyone. He owes nothing to anybody from the result of his campaign. He can keep his promises, and that is a big difference that many have ignored, especially the media after Trump won. To most of us that means Trump can govern, and he can lead America without owing the swamp. Will Congress let Trump be Trump? I think that is a resistance on the part of Congress. They are upset that Trump is not beholden to some of the people Congress is beholden to. The true objective of the United States of America is now strength and not popularity. Faced with the rest of the world, we have no choice. In many ways the rest of the world has neutralized the United States. Advanced technology or military might will not save us. Only leadership, courage, the American spirit, and freedom can save us from losing not only our democracy but also our way of life.

CHAPTER 15

Making America Great Again

LEADERS NEVER GIVE UP, AND they never give in. They understand the mission at hand and the direction to complete the mission. Even though they get faced with a truckload of items, they ultimately can see the priorities. That skill of being able to target the priorities over the clutter is not just a skill, it is a talent. Trump's first priority that he jumped on and would not be refused was appointing a Supreme Court justice. Bill Moyer, longtime news professional broadcaster from PBS broadcast network, was quoted, "Above all, it means judges with a political agenda, appointed for life, will shape America more than any other area of our government and determine history." This could be a very accurate statement for the Trump presidency. It appears that Trump will appoint at least two Supreme Court justices and has already appointed countless circuit court judges to the bench. The different areas that Trump can effect change in the United States are quite remarkable. His decisions and direct orders to the executive branch of the federal government are having a lasting impact on how the United States will be run as a nation going forward.

Starting with his own White House, something that is not being reported by NBC news, ABC news, CBS news, MSNBC news, CNN, or even FOX news had reported this as of late July 2017. The Trump White House has saved US taxpayers quite a bit of money. On July 21, 2017, The Trump administration released its annual report to Congress on White House office personnel. It includes the name, salary, and position title of all 377 White House employees. The report also said Trump decided not to take a dime in salary; instead he donated the salary to a great cause: the Department of the Interior, where it will be used for construction and repairs at US military cemeteries. Trump has shown a sincere passion for veterans. The report also proved that Trump is far better at saving money than Obama was. The total amount of White House salaries under Trump are $35.8 million versus $40.9 million under Obama, a savings of $5.1 million. There are 110 fewer employees on White House staff under Trump than under Obama at this point in the respective presidencies. Nineteen fewer staffers are dedicated to the first lady of the United States, FLOTUS, Melania Trump has six staffers versus twenty-four staffers dedicated to Michelle Obama, FLOTUS. Trump is working hard to change many other areas of the executive branch. Trump is making big strides in improvement of the US military, which is a very important area to make America great; as commander-in-chief, Trump has the final say-so. Trump can and will most likely decide what weapons we build, how many weapons, how many troops we recruit, and where we send these troops throughout the world. Trump can cancel contracts with Boeing, Grumman, Phillco/Ford, Hughes, Raytheon, and so on. These companies represent and are the main supplier of tanks, ships, planes, missiles, rockets, satellites, space systems, space weapons, and so on. Trump controls all military branches and the Pentagon. Trump has already ordered two attacks on Middle East areas, and be certain, there will be more to come. The next big thing for Trump will be North Korea. The fact that ISIS has been extracted from Mosul, Iraq, will be another positive notch for Trump. Remember when Obama pulled out all US troops from Iraq in 2011? That is when ISIS grew and went from the JV team to the number one and largest terror army in the world. Chief of Staff General "Mad Dog" Mattis has become their worst nightmare, and now success is finally taking place against ISIS.

WHAT HAS PRESIDENT DONALD TRUMP DONE IN HIS FIRST SEVEN MONTHS IN OFFICE?
Call it the "nifty fifty":

1. Appointed Supreme Court Justice Neal Gorsuch
2. Took the United States out of the Trans-Pacific Partnership, TPP

3. Illegal immigration has now dropped 70 percent, the lowest in seventeen years
4. Attacked Syrian airbase with fifty-nine Tomahawk missiles.
5. Consumer confidence highest since 2000 at the index of 125.6
6. Mortgage application for new homes has risen to a seven-year high.
7. Increased the tariff on Canadian lumber from 7 percent to 24 percent
8. Pulled us out of the very costly Paris Climate Accord, saving us billions of dollars that would go to other countries as well
9. Approved the Keystone Pipeline
10. NATO allies agreed to boost their spending by 4.3 percent
11. Rewrote the enforcement laws on the Veterans Administration and allowed the agency to fire employees who show neglect or mishandling of patient care
12. Allowed for private health-care choices for veterans
13. Over seven hundred thousand new jobs created
14. Median household income at a seven-year high.
15. Stock market at an all-time high: Dow Jones has gone up 22 percent since Trump took office in just seven months
16. $89 billion saved in the United States so far in regulation rollbacks
17. China agrees to allow import of US beef
18. Trump drops the M.O.A.B. bomb on ISIS
19. Rollback of regulation a to boost coal mining.
20. Executive order to repeal the Johnson Amendment
21. NASA moving again and taking on more significant projects.
22. $600 million cut from the UN peacekeeping budget
23. MS-13, the dangerous street gang, is being rounded up and put in prison
24. Violent illegal immigrants are being deported in record numbers
25. Signed forty-three bills to date
26. Created a commission to stop child trafficking
27. Created a commission to investigate voter fraud and abuse
28. Created a commission for opioids addiction
29. Has given legal power to individual states to drug test those collecting unemployment checks

30. Unemployment hits a sixteen-year low
31. Created the "Women in Entrepreneurship Act"
32. Reversed Dodd-Frank
33. Created the office for illegal crime victims
34. Ended the DAPA program
35. Has reversed corporations from moving out of the United States
36. Toyota is building huge manufacturing plant in the United States
37. Putting consumers and businesses to once again hire American and buy American
38. Cutting regulations on a ratio never before seen in the United States; cutting 2 regulations for every one created
39. Reviewing all trade agreements to make sure they benefit "America First"
40. Major US reinvestment commitments from Exxon/Mobil, Bayer, Apple, SoftBank, and Toyota for a total of $78 billion promised
41. Highest manufacturing surge in the last four years
42. Saves at least $22 million in the White House payroll
43. Saves the federal government millions by denying a new FBI building
44. Renegotiates the Air Force F-35 contract; saves $700 million
45. Department reports a $182 billion surplus for April 2017, the second-largest budget surplus in history
46. Signed an executive order to promote energy independence and economic growth
47. Refused to take the presidential paycheck, instead donated it to improve the surrounding areas of the veterans' grave sites located throughout the United States
48. Negotiated the release of six US humanitarian workers held captive in Egypt
49. Worked with Congress to pass more legislation in the first 7 months that any other president since Truman
50. Has given a directive to each of the executive branches under the presidency a six-month time frame to trim the fat, restructure, and improve efficiency of their branch; directive was given on March 15, 2017

The facts are in! Trump put together the strongest working team possibly of all time. The selected members in his cabinet and the key positions of the executive branch have been highly qualified and successful. The atmosphere of success is important because his team has been around success and doing something that creates value. Politicians and their staff members do not often create value. The picks that Trump selected have been in business or have been pro-business, and that has made all the difference. The Trump White House staff, on the other hand, has been a different story. Trump has an inexperienced and much weaker crew. The reason the White House staff is weaker is they lack the years of political exposure, and they are trying to play the game straight up. What does it mean to play it straight up? It means to be transparent. The Obama Administration played the game a different way, namely, tell everyone we are going to be highly transparent and then turn around and keep everything secret. The Barack Obama presidency was the least transparent in modern times with the exception of the Nixon administration. There will be many future changes to the White House staff, and Trump needs to be very careful who he relies on. It can be a dangerous political situation if he has the wrong people working in his inter most circle. The president of the United States has the authority to nominate members of his or her cabinet to the US Senate for confirmation under appointments clause of the US Constitution.

You Win with People
Trump's Top Team Members

Michael Pence, Vice President of the United States: There are still many registered voters who do not agree with Mike Pence and his policies; he did sponsor a very conservative bill in his state called the Religious Freedom Restoration Act, which made most liberals go crazy. He also initiated in 2013 the largest Indiana tax cut in history. It is most likely, percentagewise, the unregistered nonvoters who disagree with his conservative views. He stands for and has been speaking out on conservative topics like, secure borders, gun protection rights, limits on immigration, reducing government regulations, and repeal and replace Obamacare. He has his detractors, but all-in-all Mike Pence is possibly the best vice-president pick Trump could have made for now and in the future. Mike Pence is trustworthy, and there is no current or past evidence in his background that would refute those facts. It is quite important that he is viewed as trustworthy because the Trump family is vilified by many as not being trustworthy. History will show one day that the MSM and the liberals got this perception all wrong about the Trump family, but for now, this negative perception is here for a while and perhaps will be the case through his entire time in office. The media is not slowing down on the Trump attacks, and neither are the liberals who will never accept Trump.

Anyway back to vice-president Pence. Michael Edward Pence was born June 7, 1959, in Columbus, Indiana; his mother is Nancy Jane Pence, and his father is Richard J. Pence. He has five brothers and sisters. He went to local schools growing up and attended and graduated from Hanover College of Indiana with a bachelor's degree in history in 1981 and his JD degree from Indiana University's Robert H McKinney School of Law in 1986. Since that time Mike Pence has served in the state legislator and the US congress. Pence was elected Indiana governor in 2012. Pence is strong family man with strong Christian values. He has led a modest Midwestern lifestyle and is a stark contrast to Donald Trump. When the Trump campaign went on their search for a vice-president pick, the strategy must have been: Let's find someone who is the opposite of Donald Trump. Not been married three times, not been an ex-playboy, not been on television, not been involved with national and international beauty pageants, not been a world jet-setter, and not been a celebrity like Trump. Pence is and will continue to be a steady rock who supports Trump and makes him come out looking fine in the long run. His demeanor is an absolute off-set to the Trump personality. When the Trump remarks get everyone hot and bothered, Pence comes along with the calming words of wisdom and the Rodney King attitude, "Can't we just all get along?" The American people just expect negative situations and missteps from Trump, but Pence seems to never really make mistakes or say the wrong thing. He is also doing more than the average vice-president. Trump has placed him in charge of important projects. This will also be positive for the Trump administration in the long run.

Rex Tillerson, US secretary of state. Rex Wayne Tillerson is the sixty-ninth US secretary of State, confirmed on February 1, 2017. Rex was born on March 3, 1952, in Wichita Falls, Texas. He is the son of Patty Sue Tillerson and Bobby Joe Tillerson. Rex became an Eagle Scout in 1965, and from 2001 to 2012, he was the national president of the Boy Scouts of America. His father was an executive with the Boy Scouts, and this led to the Tillersons move to Huntsville, Texas. He graduated from Huntsville high school in 1970. He was the leader of the percussion section in his high-school band. He played the snare drum and kettle drums. He earned spots in the all-regional bands in his senior year. He received his bachelor of science degree in civil engineering from the University of Texas at Austin in 1975. Rex married twice and divorced his first wife, with whom he has twin boys. He married Renda St. Clair in 1986; she has a son from a previous marriage. Rex and Renda had another son together, born in 1988. Tillerson's twin sons both have engineering bachelors' degrees from the University of Texas at Austin where Rex went to school. Rex became the CEO of the world's largest publicly traded oil and gas company, ExxonMobil. Rex joined Exxon in 1975 right after graduation and rose to the top of the organization. In a 2015 *Forbes* magazine article, Tillerson was named the twenty-fifth most powerful man in the United States. His net worth is estimated at $245 million. Tillerson has a background as a global dealmaker. Trump invited Tillerson to a meeting without giving him an exact reason for the meeting. Tillerson assumed that the meeting was to discuss the global energy picture and how America could be oil independent. Instead Trump offered him the job as secretary of state. Tillerson was taken aback with the offer but nevertheless took the job. He has been vilified by the left for having relationships with Russians. It would have to be understood that oil and gas exploration and production is a worldwide endeavor. Many countries, almost all countries, have been sharing technology and projects since the end of World War II. During his time at Exxon, Mr. Tillerson forged multibillion-dollar deals with Russia's state oil company, Rosneft, including an agreement to explore the oil resources in Siberia that could be worth billions of dollars. Tillerson has also been criticized for having a business relationship with Igor Sechin, Rosneft's executive chairman who was formerly Mr. Putin's deputy prime minister. Mr. Sechin has been called Russia's second most powerful man behind Putin. Remember the old saying, "Keep your friends Close and your enemies closer"? For our state department and for the interests of the United States, who would be better to deal with the Russians than someone who knows the Russians and how they operate? It is the most logical path and really a brilliant move on the part of Trump. Tillerson will prove, in the long run, to be the absolute best pick for US secretary of state. Tillerson beat out a long list of qualified candidates for SOTUS, including former Massachusetts Governor and former Republican presidential nominee Mitt Romney, Senator Bob Corker from Ohio, and former CIA director David Petraeus.

General James Norman "Mad Dog" Mattis: He is the twenty-sixth and current US secretary of defense. Mattis retired after forty-one years of military service and was the commander of the US Central Command. In his previous position, General Mattis was in charge of American military operations in the Middle East, Northeast Africa, and Central Asia beginning in August 11, 2010, and ending in March 22, 2013. President Barack Obama decided to force the marine corps legend out early because the civilian officials and the Pentagon lawyers were rubbed the wrong way by Mattis. General Mattis was asked to leave his office in January 2013, several months earlier than planned. Mattis was considered too hawkish by the Obama administration standards. Mattis also replaced General David Petraeus in 2010, and he was appointed by Obama. Mattis has been very critical of former president Obama, especially in recent years, and is not a fan of Obama. He challenged and objected to Obama's Iran policy and the Iran nuclear deal.

James Mattis was born on September 8, 1950, in Pullman, Washington. He is the son of Lucille Mattis and John West Mattis, an ex-merchant mariner. His mother actually worked in army intelligence in South Africa for Canada as a Canadian citizen during the early part of World War II. The family eventually moved to Richland, Washington, and John Mattis went to work at a plant providing fissile material to the Manhattan Project, for the building of the first atomic bomb. James Mattis was raised in a household that did not allow television. He was raised in a bookish environment, making him a good student. He earned a BA degree in history from Central Washington University in 1971. He later earned a master of arts degree in international security affairs from the National War College in 1994. James initially enlisted in the marine corps reserves in 1969 He was commissioned as a second lieutenant. As a lieutenant, Mattis served in the rifle and weapons platoon commander in the third marine division. As a promoted captain, he was assigned as the Naval Academy Preparatory School as battalion officer and commanded rifle and weapons companies in the first marine regiment and then promoted to major. Mattis is a graduate of the US Marine Corps Amphibious Warfare School and also a graduate of the National War College. During the first Persian Gulf war, Mattis was promoted to the rank of lieutenant colonel and commanded the First Battalion, Seventh Marines. During the initial planning for the war in Afghanistan, Mattis led Task Force 58 in operations, now promoted to brigadier general, becoming the first marine corps officer to ever command a naval task force in combat. As a major general, Mattis commanded the First Marine Division in the Iraq invasion in 2003. This would give Mattis over eleven years of combat experience. Often military leaders do not see actual combat. This is not the case with General "Mad Dog" Mattis. Mattis is not allowing the bureaucrats to slow him down, and in fact, he is cleaning house at the Pentagon. Reports say that he is firing numerous attorneys who have bogged down the military from doing their job out in the battlefields where it counts.

Mad Dog Mattis famous quotes:

1. "I come in peace; I didn't bring artillery. But I'm pleading with you, with tears in my eyes: If you fuck with me, I'll kill you all."
2. "Marines don't know how to spell the word defeat."
3. "Be polite, be professional, but have a plan to kill everybody you meet."
4. "I don't lose any sleep at night; I keep others awake at night."
5. "The first time you blow someone away is not an insignificant event. That said, there are some assholes in the world that just need to be shot."
6. "Fight with a happy heart and a strong spirit."
7. "Demonstrate to the world there is 'No better Friend, No Worse Enemy' than a US Marine."
8. "I'm going to plead with you, do not cross us. Because if you do, the survivors will write about what we do here for 10,000 years."
9. "You go into Afghanistan, you got guys who slap women around for five years because they didn't wear a veil. You know, guys like that ain't got no manhood left anyway. So it is a hell of a lot of fun to shoot them. Actually it's quite fun to fight them, you know. It's a hell of a hoot. It's fun to shoot some people. I'll be right up there with you. I like brawling."
10. "You cannot allow any of your people to avoid the brutal facts. If they start living in a dream world, it's going to be bad."
11. "There is nothing better than getting shot at and missed; it is great feeling."

My personal favorite from Mad Dog: "Find the enemy that wants to end this experiment [in American democracy] and kill every one of them until they're so sick of the killing that they leave us and our freedoms intact."

If the United States falls under attack, or we go to war again, then the commander we will want leading us in the fight is General "Mad Dog" Mattis.

The Final Duty

The soldier turned to face his God,
Which must always come to pass.
He hoped his shoes were shining
Just as smartly as his brass.

"Step forward now, you soldier.
How should I deal with you?
Have you always turned the other cheek?
And to your church have you been true?"

The soldier squared his jaw and said,
"No Lord, I guess I ain't.
For those of us who carry guns
Can't always be a saint

"I had to work most Sundays,
And at times my talk was tough.
Didn't always turn the other cheek,
Because the world gets mighty rough.

"I didn't pass a cry for help
Among the chosen people here.
They never really wanted me around
Except to calm their fears.

"If you could spare a place for me,
It need not be so grand.
If I make heaven nervous,
Then I will understand."

There was silence all around heaven,
Where the saints now often trod,
As the soldier quietly waited
For the judgment of his God.

"Step forward now, you soldier.
You've carried your burdens well.
Walk peacefully on heaven's streets;
You've served your time in HELL."
—By Mitchell Morrison

Jeff Sessions: He is the eighty-fourth attorney general of the United States. Jefferson Beauregard Sessions III was born December 24, 1946, in Selma, Alabama. Jeff is what we may call "vertically challenged," that is, he is short! He stands five feet four inches tall and also, compared to some of Trump's other team members, he is short in financial capital. Basically, his family is of modest net worth, with $7.5million. This is in still in the top 1 percent of all Americans, but compared to Tillerson and Trump billionaires, it is a modest sum. General Mattis is the least wealthy of the Trump cabinet. Jefferson Sessions was named after his father, who was named after his grandfather. They all were named after Jefferson Davis, the president of the Confederate States of America, and P. G. T. Beauregard, the confederate general who commanded the bombardment of Fort Sumter, starting the American Civil War. The Sessionses are of Scots-Irish decent. In 1964 Jeff Sessions became an Eagle Scout in the Boy Scouts of America, earning the same award that Rex Tillerson also received. He attended high school at Wilcox County High School in nearby Camden, Alabama. He graduated with a BA degree in 1969. Sessions attended the University of Alabama School of Law and graduated with a JD degree in 1973. He entered private law practice in Russellville, Alabama, and later in Mobile, Alabama. He served in the army reserve in the 1970s with the rank of captain. He and his wife Mary have three children and six grandchildren.

Steven Mnuchin: He took office as the secretary of the US Treasury on February 13, 2017. Steven Terner Mnuchin was born on December 21, 1962, in New York City. He is the second youngest son of a Jewish family, Robert E. Mnuchin and Elaine Terner Cooper, who currently reside in Washington, Connecticut. Mnuchin attended Riverdale Country School in New York City. He then attended Yale University and graduated in 1985 with a bachelor's degree. At Yale, Mnuchin was publisher of the *Yale Daily News* and was also in initiated into the famous (or infamous) Skull and Bones secret society club in 1985. Mnuchin was an intern at Soloman Brothers Investment Banking Firm in New York City. However, after he graduated from Yale in 1985, he joined Goldman Sachs, where his father had worked since 1957. Mnuchin started in the mortgage department and became a partner at Goldman in 1994. He left the company in 2002 after seventeen years of employment. He left with an estimated $46 million of company stock and also $12.6 million in cash compensation. In 2009 he formed Indy Mac, a mortgage lender that came under fire during the mortgage crisis. They eventually changed the name to One West Bank. Mnuchin has also been an executive producer in Hollywood on the following major motion pictures: *The Lego Movie, Winter's Tale, Edge of Tomorrow, This Is Where I leave You, Annabelle, Inherent Vice, American Sniper, Run All Night, Get Hard, Mad MAX Fury Road, Entourage, Vacation, The Man from U.N.C.L.E., Black Mass, The Intern, Pan, Our Brand Is Crisis, In the Heart of the Sea, How to Be Single, Midnight Special, Batman v. Superman: Dawn of Justice, Keanu, The Conjuring 2, Central Intelligence, The Legend of Tarzan, Lights Out, Suicide Squad, Sully, Storks, The Accountant, Rules Don't Apply, Collateral Beauty, The Lego Batman Movie, Fist Fight, CHIPS, King Arthur: Legend of the Sword, Wonder Woman, The Lego Ninjago Movie,* and *The Disaster Artist.* He was perhaps the most active executive producer up until he was appointed as the Secretary. I think you get the picture with Steven Mnuchin; he is very wealthy and very experienced in finance and lending. The role of the secretary of the US Treasury is considered one of the top five positions in the presidential cabinet. The secretary of the Treasury must be confirmed by the Senate Committee on finance first and then confirmed by the Senate by majority vote of sixty Senators. The secretary of the Treasury is actually fifth in line for presidential succession. If anything happens to the POTUS, then the vice-president is next, followed by the speaker of the House, the secretary of state, and then the secretary of the Treasury. The secretary of the Treasury is the principal economic advisor to the president and plays a critical role in policy making. The secretary is responsible for formulating and recommending domestic and international financial, economic, and tax policy. The office will also be responsible for broad fiscal policies and managing the public debt. The Department of Treasury is the financial agent for the US government and in manufacturing coins and currency. The secretary of the Treasury is chairman of the boards and managing trustee of the Social Security and Medicare Trust Funds, also is US governor of the International Monetary Fund, The International Bank for Reconstruction and Development, the Inter-American Development Bank, the Asian Development Bank, and the European Bank for Reconstruction and Development. The Department of the Treasury was responsible up until 2003 for law-enforcement agencies that have since been reassigned to the Department of Homeland Security. Those agencies were US Customs Service; the Bureau of Alcohol, Tobacco, Firearms, and Explosives (ATF); and the US Secret Service.

David Shulkin: He is the secretary of Veterans Affairs and took office on February 13, 2017; he was unanimously confirmed by the Senate. His political party is independent, and he served under the Obama administration as the undersecretary of Veterans Affairs for Health of the United States Department of Veterans Affairs from 2015 until 2017. David Jonathon Shulkin was born at a military base in Fort Sheridan, Illinois, on July 22, 1959. Fort Sheridan is in the Highland Park area of Illinois. His father was the army psychiatrist. He is married to Merle Bari, also a physician and dermatologist. David Shulkin received his BA from Hampshire college in 1982 and an MD degree from Medical College of Pennsylvania (which has since merged into Drexel University). He did his internship at Yale School of Medicine and his residency and fellowship in General Medicine at the University of Pittsburg. In his increasing role as the new secretary of Veterans Affairs, Shulkin has sprung into action. In his most recent proactive visit to a VA hospital on August 4, 2017, Shulkin fired the third Veterans Administration hospital official. He visited the Manchester, New Hampshire, VA Medical center on a Friday. Friday is the most popular day to get fired, at least according to US figures. Shulkin announced he was removing the head of nursing services, the third leader and a total of three fired from the same facility. Shulkin was acting in response to over a dozen whistle-blowers currently and formerly employed by the hospital. The whistle-blowers reported substandard care and abuses. Two of the whistle-blowers were the recently retired chief of medicine and the former chief of surgery, and they pointed out a variety of deficiencies ranging from flies in an operating room to spine surgery patients permanently disabled as a result of neglect. Shulkin met privately with eight of the whistle-blowers on Friday August 4, 2017. Shulkin also announced that his department planned to invest $30 million in the hospital in order to improve care. It is a proven fact that under the Obama administration, the VA hospitals were a mess, in violation of federal law and dangerous places for our veterans to receive their primary health care. Shulkin is making a huge difference, and we all must say it is about time we focused on this vital area. It was a disgrace to our servicemen and women to let things get so bad under the Obama administration.

Alex Acosta: The US secretary of labor took office April 28, 2017. He was confirmed by the US Senate on a sixty-to-thirty-eight member vote; eight Democrats voted for the confirmation. He is the twenty-seventh secretary of labor. Acosta is a Republican and Hispanic. He was previously appointed by President George W. Bush to the National Labor Relations Board and later served as assistant attorney general for civil rights. He was also the former dean of Florida International College of Law. Acosta's full name is Rene Alexander Acosta. He was born on January 16, 1969, in Miami, Florida. He is the son of Cuban immigrants. He is a native of Miami, where he attended the Gulliver private schools. He went on to Harvard University and received a BA in economics in 1990, and then he graduated cum laude from Harvard University Law School in 1994. He became the second dean of

Florida International University College of Law. During Acosta's tenure, FIU has risen to #100 in the US News and World Report Rankings. Acosta has twice been named one of the most influential Hispanics by *Hispanic Business Magazine*. Acosta has an important role for several reasons. Reason 1: Acosta oversees the Pension Benefit Guarantee Corporation, which insures pension benefits for forty million Americans. Reason 2: Drastic changes were enacted under the Obama administration with Secretary of Labor Tom Perez, a Democrat. Under Tom Perez the Department of Labor took on the task of worker's retirement plans. Basically in their misguided effort to assist retirement plans with workers located in the United States. This was a great overreach in the sense that the federal government would now supervise, through new rules, the retirement accounts, and the financial advisors who give financial advice would now be held out as fiduciaries. A fiduciary is a legal designation of someone who is legally responsible for stewardship. The intent of the fiduciary rules are now based on "putting the clients first." This is what does happen with legitimate financial advice and true professionals. These rules now mean that if a financial advisor, who charges any fees for this service or participates in any commissions, and has a choice of making a decision on behalf of a retirement account, then those investment choices must be in the best interest of the client over all else. This is already in place in the United States, and it is heavily reinforced at many levels with all financial services firms. Currently the financial industry and the area of offering financial choices is regulated by at least four agencies or organizations. The largest US government group is the SEC, headquartered in Washington, DC, which regulates almost all investments, public and private. The SEC not only can shut down bad investment firms and bad advisors, they can and do bring criminal charges. Bernie Madoff comes to mind for running a Ponzi scheme that took billions from investors. Next there is FINRA, Financial Regulatory Association. FINRA has currently 3,500 employees, and they regulate approximately 620,000 licensed financial advisors and approximately 2,800 financial firms. FINRA has the authority to audit any financial licensed office at any time and visit those offices unannounced. FINRA sends out into the home offices and the individual personal offices with the thousands of their enforcement employees into the field five days a week throughout the entire year except the month of December. FINRA does shut down for that month. Also each of the fifty US states has a state securities division for enforcement, and each state has its own Department of Insurance that regulates all life, health, fixed and variable annuities, and long-term care insurance. What the Department of Labor fiduciary rule has created is a way to make trial lawyers richer and now able to sue the financial advisor if they can claim an advisor did not "place the client first." The effect has already surfaced, because if you have a retirement account like a 401(k) or Individual Retirement Account (IRA), Roth IRA or pension and profit sharing plans, Defined Benefit or Defined Contribution retirement plans, all of these accounts are subject to the Department of Labor fiduciary rules. The backlash to all retirement clients is that now all of us can expect higher annual administrative fees. These fees will either be directly charged to each individual participant and deducted from the account each year, or the fees will be hidden and then affect net returns and annual distributions to each account. All financial firms have had to beef up their staff of people to keep up with this massive regulation policy. The Trump administration has dropped the ball in this important area, and I must be critical at this point. This was an important area that has escaped the Trump wisdom.

Rick Perry: United States Secretary of Energy Perry took office on March 2, 2017, as the fourteenth US secretary of energy. Perry was also a presidential candidate opposing Donald Trump in the Republican primaries, but Perry had an early exit when his poll numbers were just too low. James Richard Perry was born on March 4, 1950, in Haskel, Texas. He is the second-born son of tenant farmers and raised in the tiny West Texas community of Paint Creek. His parents are Joseph Ray and Amelia June Holt Perry, and he has an older sister. His family dates back to the original thirteen colonies, and his family has been in Texas since the Texas Revolution. His father was a registered Democrat and was a longtime Haskell County commissioner and school board member. Rick Perry even started out as a registered Democrat. Growing up, Rick was in the Boy Scouts of America. He was active in scouting and earned distinction as an Eagle Scout. Perry graduated from Paint Creek High School in 1986. He was one of the first of his family members to go to college. He attended Texas A&M University and received a bachelor's degree in animal science; he was a member of the Corps of Cadets and a Yell Leader. Between 1972 and 1977, Perry served in the US Air Force, flying C-130 tactical airlift aircraft in the Middle East and Europe. Rick married his childhood sweetheart, Anita Thigpen Perry, in 1982. They have two children and two granddaughters. Perry grew up in the United Methodist Church. He and his family were members of the Terrytown United Methodist Church in Austin, Texas, until 2010 when they began attending Lake Hills Church. Lake Hills is a nondenominational Evangelical megachurch in western Travis County, Texas. Perry became dramatically more religious, and in June 2011, Perry proclaimed August 6 as a day of prayer and fasting in the state of Texas. Perry was not always a Republican. In 1988 Perry supported Al Gore for president in the Democratic primaries and worked in an unspecified capacity for Gore's campaign in Texas. In September 1989, Perry announced he was switching political parties, becoming a Republican. Prior to being elected as Texas's lieutenant governor in 1998, he served two terms as Texas commissioner of agriculture and three terms in the Texas House of Representatives. Perry was the forty-seventh governor and the longest-serving governor in Texas history, having led the world's twelfth-largest economy. During his tenure, he took Texas through a record growth spurt from 2000 until 2015. He devoted those fifteen years to creating prosperity and opportunity for Texas families. He added 2.2 million jobs during his time in office. Perry was a candidate for president of the United States but dropped his run for POTUS on September 11, 2015. Perry was just too far behind in the polls and had major difficulty raising the necessary funds. He quickly endorsed Donald Trump over fellow Texas Republican Ted Cruz. With his position as secretary of the Department of Energy, Perry has an important job because the Department of Energy, although often criticized for doing nothing, is in charge of the safety and security of the nuclear power plants and all the power grids. These are the responsibility of the Department of Energy. The department itself has a robust security protection team for counterterrorism. One of the major ways a hostile country could hurt the United States is to take down our power grids. For that matter, organized terror groups could also do massive damage and affect millions of Americans. The situation could be quite serious and could even cause significant loss of life.

Ben Carson: The secretary of Housing and Urban Development took office March 2, 2017. Benjamin Solomon Carson was born on September 18, 1951, in Detroit, Michigan. His father was Robert Solomon Carson Jr., a World War II US Army veteran, and his mother was Sonya Carson. Robert Carson, the father, was a Baptist minister but later became a Cadillac auto plant worker. In 1950 Carson's parents purchased a new 733-square foot single-family detached home on Deacon Street in the Boynton neighborhood in southwest Detroit. Ben Carson's Detroit public school education began in kindergarten at the Fisher School and continued to the first half of the third grade. The parents divorced when Carson was eight, which led them to move to Boston and then back to Detroit without the father. Carson attended the predominantly black Southwestern High School of Detroit in the ninth through twelfth grades. Carson's SAT college admission test scores ranked him in the ninetieth percentile, and a *Detroit Free Press* article stated, "Carson Gets Highest SAT Scores in Twenty Years" of any student in Detroit public schools. He decided to apply to Yale for two reasons. First, he only had ten dollars to apply for one college application fee, and second, he decided to apply to Yale University after seeing a team from Yale defeat a team from Harvard on the *GE College Bowl* television show. Carson was accepted by Yale and offered a full scholarship covering tuition, room, and board. Carson graduated with a BA in psychology from Yale in 1973. He entered the University of Michigan Medical School in 1973. He struggled academically in the beginning, but by his second year, he began to excel. Carson graduated from the University of Michigan Medical School with an MD in 1977 and was accepted to the Alpha Omega Alpha Honor Medical Society. Carson was then accepted by the Johns Hopkins University School of Medicine neurosurgery program in Baltimore, Maryland. He was the director of pediatric neurosurgery at Johns Hopkins from 1984 until his retirement in 2013. He was a pioneer in neurosurgery; his achievements include performing the only successful separation of conjoined twins joined at the back of the head. He pioneered the first successful neurosurgical procedure on a fetus inside the womb, performing the first completely successful separation of type-2 vertical craniopagus twins. He became the youngest chief of pediatric neurosurgery in the country at the age of thirty-three. He has received more than sixty honorary doctorate degrees, dozens of national merit citations, and written over one hundred neurosurgical publications. In 2008 he was bestowed the Presidential Medal of Freedom, the highest civilian award in the United States. On May 4, 2015, he announced he was running for the Republican nomination in the 2016 presidential elections; in March 2016, following the Super Tuesday primaries, he suspended his campaign and announced he would endorse the candidacy of Donald Trump. Ben is married to Larcena "Candy" Rustin. They met in 1971 as students at Yale University. They were married in 1975 and lived in Howard County, Maryland. Together they have three sons, Rhoeyce, Benjamin Jr., and Murray.

Housing and Urban Development, or HUD, has a long history in the US government, dating back to 1934. The department name was given by President Lyndon Johnson to develop and execute policies and metropolises on September 9, 1965. The milestones of HUD include:

- The National Housing Act, June 27, 1934. Provided mortgage insurance on loans from FHA approved lenders.
- The Housing Act of 1937, which helps enact slum-clearance projects and construction of low-rent housing.
- The National Mortgage Association (FNMA) was created February 3, 1938.
- In 1968 The Fair Housing Act was created to ban discrimination in housing.
- In August 1974, the Housing and Community Development Act of 1974 allows community development block grants and help for urban homesteading.

- On October 1977, The Housing and Community Act of 1977 set up Urban Development Grants and continues elderly and handicapped assistance.

Overall HUD continues to evolve and meet the needs of Americans with home ownership and the challenge of keeping Americans in safe, comfortable residences.

Sonny Perdue: The US secretary of agriculture took office April 25, 2017. Previously Sonny served as the eighty-first governor of Georgia from 2013 to 2011. Upon his inauguration as governor on January 13, 2003, he became the first Republican governor of Georgia since Reconstruction after the Civil War. He is the thirty-first agriculture secretary and was confirmed by a vote of eighty-seven to eleven in his favor on April 24, 2017.

Sonny was born December 20, 1946, in Perry Georgia. His birth name is George Ervin Sonny Perdue III, the son of Ophie Viola Holt a teacher and George Ervin Perdue Jr., a farmer. He grew up in Bonaire, an unincorporated area between Perry and Warner Robbins, Georgia. He prefers to be called Sonny and signs the official documents as Sonny. Perdue is also the first cousin of US Senator David Perdue. Perdue grew up in the local town and played quarterback at Warner Robbins High School and was a walk-on at the University of Georgia football team. He was also a member of the Kappa Sigma Fraternity. Perdue served in the US Air Force rising to the rank of Captain before his discharge. In 1971 Perdue earned his doctor of veterinary medicine (DVM) from the University of Georgia and worked as a veterinarian before becoming a small business owner, eventually starting three small businesses. Perdue and his wife, Mary Ruff, were married in 1972 after dating for four years. They have four children (Leigh, Lara, Jim, and Dan) and have fourteen grandchildren (six boys and eight girls). They have also been foster parents for many children. They still live in Bonaire, Georgia. Perdue ran as a Democrat in 1990 as a state senator in the eighteenth district. He defeated Republican Ned Sanders. He switched party affiliation from Democrat to Republican and was reelected as a Republican in 1998 and also reelected in 2000. In December 2001, Perdue resigned as state senator and devoted his time to running for the office of governor of Georgia. He won the 2002 election, defeating Roy Barnes 51–46 percent. Perdue advocated reforms to cut waste in the state government. In 2003 Perdue signed an executive order prohibiting himself and all other state employees from accepting any gift over twenty-five dollars. Perdue took an inventory of the sales of Georgia's surplus vehicles and real estate. Prior to Perdue becoming governor, no state agency had even compiled an inventory of what assets the state owned. Perdue is known as a fiscal conservative, and he will carry this distinction to the Department of Agriculture. He is one of the more moderate in wealth. Many of Trump's cabinet members are quite successful, and politics for them would have been a distraction and a major hit to their overall wealth. The Perdue family had its last financial disclosure with his personal net worth at over $7 million dollars. Sonny is also one of Trump's three cabinet members who switched parties from Democrat to Republican in recent years.

General John F. Kelly: White House chief of staff, ex-director of Homeland Security, John Francis Kelly was born on May 11, 1950, in Boston, Massachusetts. Kelly is a retired five-star marine corps General. Kelly retired on January 14, 2016. He was appointed secretary of Homeland Security on January 20, 2017, by President Trump. At six months, Kelly's term as Secretary of Homeland Security is the shortest in in the office's history. On July 28, 2017, he was appointed to replace Reince Priebus as White House chief of staff. He took the office July 31, 2017. John Kelly grew up in the Brighton area of Boston; he enlisted in the US Marine Corps in 1970. He was discharged from active duty in 1972 as a sergeant. He entered officers' candidate school and graduated from the University of Massachusetts, Boston, as a second lieutenant in the marine corps. In 1984 He received a master of science degree in National Security Studies from the Georgetown Scholl of Foreign Service, Washington, DC. He is also a graduate in 1995 of the National War College in Washington, DC. He was promoted to major in 1984 from commanding a rifle and weapons company to a battalion operations officer. In 1987

Kelly transferred to the Basic School in Quantico, Virginia, serving first as the head of the Offensive Tactics Section and then he assumed the duties of the director of the Infantry Officer Course. Kelly has fought battles in the Persian Gulf war, the Operation Desert Storm Iraq War. He reached the duties of commanding the Southern Command on November 19, 2012, and was finally succeeded by Navy Admiral Kurt W. Tidd on January 14, 2016. Kelly is married to Karen Hernest Kelly, and they have three children.

Democrats will continue to resist—resist—resist.

Trump just needs to produce results—results—results.

1. Build the wall
2. Pass a tax bill
3. Increase jobs and the economy
4. Repeal and replace Obamacare
5. Protect us from Iran and North Korea
6. Drain the swamp

Private enterprise "Trumps" government interference and government projects every time. In the case of electric cars replacing gas-fueled cars with harmful environmental emissions, the private sector has got that all but taken care of. Private monies are pouring into these projects, and they are not taxpayer funded. Recently a company named Adomani, a Florida corporation, took its company public on the NASDAQ stock exchange. The company tripled its stock value in four weeks. Adomani is a provider of advanced zero-emission electric and hybrid vehicles and replacement drivetrains that focused the cost of ownership and reducing greenhouse gas or pollution. They design and build the drivetrains for new school buses and medium- to heavy-duty commercial vehicles. This technology breakthrough now allows these heavy vehicles to have the same power as gas or diesel-fuel vehicles. The Adomani hybrid drivetrain systems are available in both the assistive hybrid format and the full traction format for use in private and commercial fleet vehicles of all sizes. This company is going to place large trucks and buses on the road with zero emissions. Trump knows about this kind of thing, and he does not have to use taxpayer dollars to make it happen. If fact, he does not have to slash regulations, either, because the new electric vehicles meet the Environmental Protection Agency (EPA) Tier 4 emissions standards, and it meets the California Air Resources Board (CARB) regulations—even the "Republic of California" agrees with that. Trump is really "getting his cake and eating it too"; the private sector is solving the climate change solution of lowering greenhouse gases. New inventions and switching to nonpolluting cars are making an impact. Trump does not have to really do anything at this point in the history of his presidency. He can sit back and let the statistics speak for themselves. He could be looking really good by 2020 because cars, buses, and trucks are going to be on the roads across the United States and no longer polluting the air we breathe.

The Trump Bump

On July 31 the American Institute of CPAs sent out a report on a survey from the American public about personal financial satisfaction. The AICPA released its Q2 2017 report, and the personal financial satisfaction index has hit a ten-year high. Stock market gains, more job openings, and a decrease in inflation drove personal financial satisfaction. Not since the fourth quarter of 2006 has the index been this favorable. On the same day, the Dow Jones Industrial averages hit an all-time high at 21,898, and then on July 2, 2017, the Dow closed at 22,016. This rise in the stock market is very impressive; in November 2016, one day before the election of President Trump, the Dow was at 18,259. This rise could also indicate that the Dow Jones has risen over 22 percent in just seven months and eighteen days. It was not known by the stock markets until November 10 that Trump had won the election; after that date, the markets took off on this historical rise. There are many specific reasons that the stock market is up in value. Reason 1: Trump is making it more profitable to do business in the United States. Trump has eliminated regulations that were hostile to corporate profits. By getting rid on hundreds of regulations, business can keep more of the profits and lower their overhead and even legal costs to deal with the regulations. Reason 2: Trump has promised to lower the corporate tax rate for business in the United States, and much of Congress has committed to that promise. Business has anticipated that fact, so those businesses are increasing their research and development and investing more capital to increase production and new innovations. Reason 3: The new pro-business climate is keeping US companies from moving overseas and therefore bringing back jobs, and that helps the overall economy. It appears to working because on August 4, the Department of Labor reported that the business added 209,000 workers to the labor force, again beating the forecasts. The unemployment rate ticked down from 4.4 percent in June 2017 to 4.3 percent in July 2017. This matched an all-time low not seen since 2001, sixteen years ago. Despite all the negative news about Russia and the Trump White House, the economy is also breaking wage increase numbers. The Trump stock market bump has created around $4 trillion in added wealth to those who hold these stock positions. Those holding stocks include, but are not limited to, 401(k)s, Roth and regular IRAs, TSAs, Defined Benefit and Defined Contribution pension plans, school endowment accounts, charitable and foundation accounts, trust accounts, corporate investors, and individual investors. The extended climb in the stock market is a "tide that lifts all boats."

Who Are the Real Trumpsters?

Kellyanne Conway: Up until this point, perhaps the most loyal of all the Trump employees. Conway became Trump's final campaign manager when all others were in chaos or disorganized to the point that the election looked bleak for Donald Trump. Conway came in and brought organization to the entire campaign and was responsible for the final Trump push where he outworked Hillary four to one in number of campaign appearances in the last three weeks preceding the November election. Conway gets her hard work ethic from a very interesting personal story in her childhood days. Conway was born on January 20, 1967, in Camden New Jersey. Conway's parents divorced when she was three, and she was raised by her mother and her grandmother. She graduated from Saint Joseph High School in 1985. She was a cheerleader, played field hockey, and sang in the school choir. Her religion is Catholic. She attended Trinity College (now Trinity University) in Washington, DC, and received her BA degree in political science; she graduated magna cum laude. She went on to earn her JD with honors from George Washington University Law School in 1992. Conway has vast experience in the political arena. Among the political figures, Conway has worked for Congressman Jack Kemp, Newt Gingrich, Congressman (now vice-president) Mike Pence, Senator Fred Thompson, former vice-president Dan Quayle, and US Senate candidate Todd Akin. Conway has stepped up and helped deliver a message that would not waver, and she corrected reporters often when they would attack her candidates. She has been defending the POTUS when they would say something negative or unflattering about Trump. She now has an office on the third floor of the West Wing of the White House. Her Secret Service code name is "Blueberry." She got the nickname "Blueberry" in New Jersey at age twenty because she won the World Champion Blueberry Packing competition. She stated, "Everything I learned about life and business started on that farm and packing blueberries." She worked on that farm for eight years as a summer and part-time job. Conway is a proven hard worker and runs an extreme schedule. Since Trump was elected, Conway's schedule includes frequent weekend commutes back to her family home in Alpine, New Jersey. She is very close to Donald Trump, and she has "walk-in" privileges and can call on the president in the Oval Office unannounced. Conway has four children and is married to George T. Conway III. George is an attorney and a partner at a Manhattan-based law firm, Wachtell, Lipton, Rosen & Katz. He was considered for a post in the US Justice Department, but he withdrew his name. They plan to move to Washington, DC, in the fall; they have purchased a home located in the area near the National Cathedral area called Massachusetts Avenue Heights. The home is reported to be worth $8 million. It appears that Kellyanne is planning to assist President Trump for quite a while, at least while he is in the Oval Office. She is the best defender of POTUS Trump because she is so loyal to him at all times. She never wavers or questions Trump's decisions. I believe that her counsel to Trump is not only wise, it is more in touch with mainstream America and the things that he should focus on. Trump is very lucky; he has his own family who are "super supportive," and he now he has Kellyanne Conway.

Steven Bannon: If Kelly Ann Conway is the most loyal, then Steve Bannon maybe the most mysterious of the Trump support team. Steven Kevin Bannon is the senior counselor to the president, a position he assumed the same day Trump took office on January 20, 2017. Steve Bannon was born on November 27, 1953, in Norfolk, Virginia. His family life was modest growing up there with his mother, Doris, and father, Martin Bannon. They were a middle-class Irish Catholic family, pro-union and pro-Kennedy Democrats. Steve Bannon is now a registered Republican. Bannon attended Benedictine College Preparatory, a private Catholic, military high school in Richmond, Virginia; he graduated in 1971. After graduating from high school, Bannon attended Virginia Tech University in Blacksburg, Virginia, where he served as the president of the student government association and graduated in 1976. Steve was a US Navy officer for seven years, serving on the destroyer *USS Paul F. Foster* as a surface warfare officer in the Pacific fleet. Then he was transferred to the Pentagon. While at the Pentagon, Bannon attended Georgetown University at night and graduated with a master's degree in national security studies. He departed the navy with the rank of lieutenant (0-3). Bannon also attended Harvard University from 1983 to 1985, where he obtained his MBA with honors from Harvard Business School and graduated in 1985. Bannon settled in at a position at Goldman Sachs as an investment banker in the mergers and acquisitions department. In 1987 Bannon took advantage of Goldman's desire to expand its presence in the entertainment industry. He moved to Los Angeles for two years. In 1990 Bannon and some partners broke from Goldman Sachs and launched Bannon & Co., a boutique investment banking group specializing in media and entertainment. One of his big deals was negotiating a sale to a Ted Turner company called Castle Rock. Westinghouse Electric owned Castle Rock, which it wanted to sell. Bannon got the deal done, and CNN, the Ted Turner–owned company, made the purchase. Bannon was very smart when he took financial stakes or royalties off five television shows instead of all cash for his participation. Seinfeld was one of those shows, and to this day, every time Seinfeld airs on television, Bannon gets paid. Bannon has produced eighteen films. Bannon has received political attention because he is the founder member of the board of Breitbart News, which some consider an online far-right news, opinion, and commentary website. In March of 2012, Andrew Breitbart died, and Bannon became executive chair of Breitbart News LLC, the parent company of Breitbart News. On August 17, 2016, Bannon was appointed chief executive of Donald Trump's presidential campaign: he left Breitbart as well as the Government Accountability Institute, a conservative tax-exempt 501(C)(3) organization, to take the job as chairman of the Trump campaign. He replaced Paul Manafort. Bannon has very good skills as a strategist for the Trump administration. He is also very quiet in the background. He rarely takes television interviews and does not speak to reporters. This is why he is considered mysterious. His main function is to protect President Trump, but he also gives him advice to get his agenda done. Many times Bannon will actually run with a story for the press to focus on. When they get the information or partial information, then Bannon will advise Trump to move on another issue and get an executive order done or introduce something that normally the press would jump on. However, the press now misses the new move by Trump because they are focused on the negative or trivial story. This has happened time and again as Trump and Bannon have created diversions, and the mainstream press has missed their chance to create objection to things like immigration, sanctuary cities, and rules for the military, as a few examples. Bannon is very loyal to Trump, and he is necessary to have in Trump's corner. The mainstream media will try to throw dirt on Bannon's reputation, but other than two divorces, he has nothing in his background to smear him with.

Katrina Pierson: Since November 2015 she has been the national spokesperson for Donald Trump's 2016 presidential campaign, a regular CNN contributor, and Fox News contributor. She is Republican and was one of the original proponents of the Tea Party conservatives. She joined the Tea Party in 2008. She was born in Kansas on July 20, 1976, to a white mother and a black father. Her mother, who gave birth to her at the age of fifteen, initially gave her up for adoption but later changed her mind. Pierson was raised by her mother after father left, and she grew up in poverty. Her birth name is Katrina Lanette Shaddix. She had a three-month-long marriage at an early age and a son from that marriage. In 1997, at the age of twenty, Pierson was arrested for shoplifting at a JC Penny store in Plano, Texas. The amount was $168 in merchandise. She claimed in the courtroom that she had no money to clothe her then–three-month-old son, who was with her at the time of the arrest. She pleaded no contest, received deferred adjudication, and the case was dismissed, with the case being sealed. She took most of the JC Penny clothes for herself to go on job interviews. She has said that the incident helped her turn her life around, and she realized that doing something wrong will have consequences. After all that, she received her associate of science degree from Kilgore College, and in 2006, she earned her bachelor's degree in biology from the University of Texas at Dallas. If anyone has done a flip-flop politically, it is Katrina Pierson. She worked off and on in the medical field before she got involved in the Tea Party movement. Katrina voted for Barack Obama in 2008, stated that in the past Malcolm X was her idol, and Dr. Martin Luther King was too moderate for her. However, by April 2009, at a Dallas Tea Party event, she called for Texas to secede from the United States. She founded a local Tea Party group in Garland, Texas. In 2012, Pierson actively supported Ted Cruz in the 2012 US Senate race; she appeared onstage with him on his election night in November. Katrina ran for Congress in 2014; she challenged the incumbent Republican Congressman Pete Sessions in the primary for the Texas thirty-second district. Her run for office was endorsed by Rafael Cruz and by Sarah Palin, who called Katrina a "feisty fighter for freedom." While Senator Cruz offered some praise, he did not come out with an outright endorsement of Pierson. She lost the vote to Pete Sessions; she got 365 of the vote to Sessions's 63 percent. Pierson only raised a total of $76,000 in campaign contributions; Sessions raised twenty times that amount. After the loss, Pierson went on to become a spokesperson for the Tea Party leadership fund. In January 2015 Pierson attended a meeting for the Tea Party activists in Myrtle Beach, South Carolina, with Ted Cruz. Also while in Myrtle

Beach, she met with Donald J. Trump. She had future meetings with Trump himself and his aides; she introduced Trump at a Trump for President campaign rally held in Dallas, Texas, in September. Pierson snubbed Ted Cruz, and in November 2015, about one year before the 2016 vote for POTUS, she was hired as the national spokesperson for Trump's campaign. All through the campaign, she frequently has been a spokesperson on television and made numerous appearances on behalf of Donald Trump for President and even now, as the current presidency needs defending. Katrina, to this day, continues to be one of Trump's staunchest defenders and supporters. She has shown undying loyalty to Trump, his past reputation, and his entire family.

Dr. Sebastian Gorka: He serves as deputy assistant to the president of the United States and is a member of the national security advisory staff. Sebastian Lukacs Gorka was born October 22, 1970, in Hammersmith, London, England, to Zsuzsa Biro, mother, and Pal (Paul) Gorka, father; both parents are from Hungary. They had fled to the United Kingdom after the failed 1956 Hungarian uprising was ultimately crushed by the USSR. Gorka grew up in London and attended Saint Benedict's school in west London. He attended Heythrop College of the University of London and received a BA degree in philosophy and theology. While at the university, he joined the British Army, serving for three years in the Twenty-Second Intelligence Company of the Intelligence Security Group in the interrogation unit. This was affiliated with NATO, specializing in Russian and other languages supporting the 1 (BR) Corps. In 1992 Gorka moved to Hungary, where he worked for the Hungarian Ministry of Defense and also studied for a master's degree in international relations and diplomacy at the Budapest University of Economic Sciences, now known as Corvinus University. He completed the degree in 1997. Gorka was also a Kokkalis Fellow at the John F. Kennedy School of Government at Harvard University in the 1998–1999 academic year. In 2002 he entered the political science doctoral program at Corvinus University, completing his dissertation in 2007. Gorka worked for the Hungarian Ministry of Defense when Prime Minister Jozsef Antall was in office. Following the September 11, 2001, attacks in the United States, Gorka became a public figure in Hungary as a television counterterrorism expert. His knowledge of jihad seemed to give him credibility. He and his family relocated to the United States in 2008. He was hired as administrative dean at the National Defense University, Fort McNair, Washington, DC, where he began to lecture on irregular warfare and counterterrorism as a part of combating terrorism. From 2014 to 2016, Gorka was an editor for the Breitbart News Network, where he worked directly for Steven K. Bannon. This is his connection to the Trump campaign and the Trump presidency. Gorka has proven with his numerous television interviews that he can handle himself with the press and take on the tough questions from reporters. He is most likely going to get a leg up and win an argument with any reporter, because most reporters don't know anything about terrorism. Gorka is very loyal to Donald Trump and has a true connection to the policies and ideals of Trump; he will be a good advocate and protector of Trump in the future. Gorka is naturalized American citizen.

Corey Lewandowski: Corey was the former campaign manager for Donald J. Trump for President. Up until the last four months of the POTUS campaign, Corey was constantly by the side of Donald Trump in every campaign event or appearance. He began with Trump in January 2015, and he was fired by Trump in June of 2016. Most people are of the opinion that Donald Trump is very fond of Corey, and Trump still believes he is a super loyal devotee to Trump. That being said, Trump felt a change was necessary when he placed Corey with Kellyanne Conway as campaign manager in June 2016. This turned out to be a smart move on the part of Trump. He won the election; need I say more? Corey Lewandowski was born in Lowell, Massachusetts, on September 18, 1973. He is the grandson of a Union Printer. Lewandowski attended Lowell Catholic High School, a private college preparatory school, in the same hometown. He met his future wife, Allison, when he was in ninth grade and she was in eighth grade. However, she actually married Brian Kinney, who was Lewandowski's best friend, in 1998. Kinney died on the United Airlines Flight 176 during the September 11, 2001, terror attacks. She married Lewandowski four years after the attack, and they have four children together. After high school, in 1991, Lewandowski graduated from the University of Massachusetts at Lowell with a BA in political science. He received his MA from American University in Washington, DC, in political science. From December 1997 to February 2001, Lewandowski worked as an administrative assistant for Ohio Republican Bob Ney. In 1999, while working for Ney, Lewandowski brought a loaded handgun in a laundry bag into the Longworth House office building on Capitol Hill, Washington, DC. He was arrested and charged with a misdemeanor for bringing a handgun and ammunition into a secure federal building. Lewandowski said the whole thing was an accident. The charges eventually were dismissed. Lewandowski got his first real campaign manager job when he became the manager for US Senator Robert C. Smith of New Hampshire, challenged in the Republican primary by John E. Sununu. Sununu defeated Smith in the primary, winning 53 percent to 45 percent. Smith was the first sitting US senator in ten years to lose a primary campaign, so this was not a good start for the young Lewandowski's career as a campaign manager. Lewandowski decided to become a seasonal police officer, and he graduated from the New Hampshire Police Academy in 2006. He worked as a seasonal marine patrol office with the New Hampshire State Police from 2006 to 2010. In 2008 he began working for Americans for Prosperity, a Koch brothers–backed advocacy group. Lewandowski first met Donald Trump in April 2014 at a political event in New Hampshire, six months before Trump announced his campaign. Lewandowski was invited to Trump Tower, where he accepted an offer from the campaign to become campaign manager. His salary was $20,000 per month, which is quite modest for that large of a position on the national stage. When Lewandowski was hired, Trump had a political staff consisting of three people: his lawyer Michael D. Cohen, Roger Stone, and Paul Manafort. After a win in New Hampshire on February 9, 2016, Trump acknowledged Lewandowski's role in the win by praising his ground game.

By April 2016 Lewandowski was waning with the campaign. It was rumored that Lewandowski was clashing with Paul Manafort in an internal power struggle. Days after Lewandowski left the Trump campaign, he was hired by CNN to offer opposing views. On November 11, 2016, Lewandowski resigned as a CNN commentator amid speculations that he would be playing a role in the Trump campaign. Over the past few months, he has been an invited guest on Fox News. And he been active as a lobbyist. He has formed his own firm, Lewandowski Strategic Advisors. Corey is firmly in the corner for Donald Trump, and when he gets the opportunity, he always praises Trump and his progress in the office of the presidency.

Sheriff David Clarke: Sheriff Clarke is the current sheriff of Milwaukee County, Wisconsin. In 2002 Clarke was appointed by Governor Scott McCallum, and later he was elected that same year to his first four-year term. He was re-elected in November 2006 and is currently serving his fourth full term. Clarke is actually a registered Democrat. However, his views are staunch conservative, and he is a no-nonsense, serious man when it comes to punishing criminal behavior and criminals who dwell in our society. David Alexander Clarke Jr. was born August 21, 1956, in Milwaukee, Wisconsin. He is one of five children of Jeri and David Clarke Sr. His father was a paratrooper with the Second Ranger Infantry Company, US Army. Clarke Jr. attended Marquette University High School, where he played for the varsity basketball team. After finishing high school, Clarke took classes at the University of Wisconsin in Milwaukee but dropped out during his first year when he got a job driving beer trucks. He began his career in law enforcement in 1978 at the Milwaukee Police Department (MPD). He rose up through the ranks at a slow but steady pace in his twenty-four years in the department. Clarke was a patrol officer for thirteen years before he was promoted to homicide detective. He was promoted to lieutenant of detectives in 1993 and captain in 1999. In 1999, Clarke received a BA in management of criminal justice from Concordia University, Wisconsin's school of adult and continuing education. In 2003, Clarke received a master's degree in security studies from the Naval Postgraduate School. Clarke has had his challenges in office. In August of 2016, riots broke out in the city of Milwaukee after a fatal police shooting of twenty-three-year-old Sylville Smith. Smith, a black male, was shot by a black officer on the police force, but not the Sheriff's force. Body-camera footage later showed that Smith was holding a gun to his head. With the riots making the national news, Clarke called for the National Guard to be mobilized; he was criticized for being too aggressive. Many critics of Clarke say he went too far in his endorsements of Donald Trump. They say he has even used his office to support Trump. The symbolism of Clarke is powerful. It drives critics crazy that he is always out there wearing his sheriff's uniform and wearing the white hat; that is powerful symbolism. He has a lot of credibility with the public, and he is an outstanding communicator. The more he is ridiculed by the MSM for his incendiary remarks, the more popular he becomes. Clarke was a speaker at the Republican National Convention, and he was a huge hit. He also appears on the Fox News Network on a regular basis. Clarke has criticized Planned Parenthood and called it "Planned Genocide." He also said, "Let me tell you why blacks sell drugs and involve themselves in criminal behavior instead of a more socially acceptable lifestyle: because they are uneducated, they're lazy, and they're morally bankrupt. That why." Clarke is a frequent and outspoken critic of Black Lives Matter. He describes the movement as a hate group and calls them subhuman creeps. Clarke called former US Attorney General, Eric Holder, an asshole and accused him regarding his testimony, in front of Congress, regarding police shootings as someone who has outright hostility toward police officers.

Ann Coulter: Anne Coulter is an author and television personality who, when all is said and done, may be the biggest supporter of all the Trump supporters. She has written her own book on Donald Trump, titled *In Trump We Trust: E Pluribus Awesome*. Ann Coulter has written other very pro-conservative books, titled *Adios America*, *Mugged*, and *Never Trust a Liberal Over 3—Especially a Republican*. Ann Hart Coulter was born December 8, 1961, in New York City. Her father was John Vincent Coulter and FBI special agent of Irish German decent. Her mother was Nell Husbands. Coulter is a native of Paducah, Kentucky. Both her parents are deceased. She was raised in a conservative household and actually grew up in New Canaan, Connecticut. She has two older brothers, James and John. Ann attended Cornell University and helped found the *Cornell Review*, the school paper. She was a member of Delta Gamma sorority. She graduated cum laude from Cornell in 1984 with a BA in history. She went on to attend law school and received her JD from the University of Michigan Law School in 1988. She was also the editor of the *Michigan Law Review*. At Michigan, Coulter was president of the local chapter of the Federalist Society and was trained at the National Journalism Center. Coulter has an extensive legal background along with her writing skills. She served as a law clerk in Kansas City for Pasco Bowman II of the United States Court of Appeals for the Eighth Circuit. Coulter left to work for the US Judiciary Committee in 1994. She handled crime and immigration issues for Senator Spencer Abraham of Michigan and helped craft legislation designed to expedite the deportation of felony aliens. She is mainly known for the books that she has published. She has published twelve books and also writes a weekly syndicated newspaper column. She appears often at universities as a speaker and also appears as a favorite on the Fox News Network. She made her first national media appearance in 1996 after she was hired by the then-fledgling network MSNBC as a legal correspondent. She then began appearing on CNN and Fox News and radio talk shows also. On radio she has been featured on *American Morning, The Fifth Estate, Glenn Beck Program, The Rush Limbaugh Show, The Mike Galligher Show*, and *Real Time with Bill Maher*. On television she has appeared on the *Today Show, The View, Lou Dobbs Tonight, Fox and Friends, The O'Reilly Factor, Red Eye with Greg Gutfeld, The Sean Hannity Show, The Laura Ingraham Show, The Michael Medved Show,* and the *Tucker Carlson* show. Coulter has been engaged a few times but never married and has no children. She dated conservative writer Dinish D'Souza and has dated Andrew Stein, the former president of the New York City Council. Ann is a Christian by faith and attends church services, mainly at a Presbyterian church. Ann Coulter stood out right away when she spoke of the Trump campaign. She has continued to fight hard for Trump and was the first to go on record, just two months after his announcement that he was running for POTUS, and predict he had the best chance of winning. She said on ABC national television, "Out of all the declared seventeen candidates running for president, Donald J. Trump has the best chance of winning." This was greeted with tremendous laughter from the show's host. Coulter has a tendency to back Trump through thick and thin, and she is perhaps the liberals' worst nightmare. The liberals do often treat Ann Coulter very harshly, but nevertheless, they should respect her views and her ability to deliver an exact message. She has a very staunch conservative following and should not be underestimated. Many conservatives agree with Coulter when she calls out weak Republicans who do not back their promises. Coulter has been very critical on the fact that the Republicans have had the House the Senate and now the White House, and they cannot pass any major legislation. She is correct that the Republicans have a flawed party when they fail to stick together and cannot agree on what they promised for seven years. She will even call Trump out if he does not build the border wall. She has said time and again that building the border wall will be a promise that Trump made to the American people, and he had better keep his promise.

Newt Gingrich: Newt is an American politician, author from Georgia, and fiftieth speaker of the US House of Representatives from 1995 to 1999. He has been a big supporter of Donald Trump and acted as an adviser to the Trump POTUS 2016 campaign. Gingrich was also a Republican presidential candidate in 2012. Newton Leroy Gingrich was actually born as Newton Leroy McPherson at the Harrisburg Hospital in Harrisburg, Pennsylvania, on June 17, 1943. His mother was Kathleen Daugherty, and his father was Newton Searles McPherson. The marriage fell apart within days. In 1946, his mother married army officer Robert Gingrich, who adopted Newt, and he has used that name ever since. Most of Newt's early life was growing up on military bases in Europe and the United States. In 1961, Gingrich graduated from Baker High School in Columbus, Georgia, at Fort Benning. Newt received his BA degree in history from Emory University in Atlanta in 1965. He attended Tulane University, earning his MA in 1968 and a PhD in European history in 1971. He spent six months in Brussels, Belgium, working on his dissertation. Gingrich received military deferments from the draft during the Vietnam War years for being a student and a father. He became a teacher at the West Georgia College as an assistant professor and then as a professor. Gingrich ran for congress in the sixth district in 1974 and was defeated by Democrat incumbent Jack Flynt. Newt ran again in 1976 when Jimmy Carter was elected POTUS and was defeated for the second time. In 1978 congressman Flynt decided to retire, and Gingrich defeated Virginia Shapard by 7,500 votes. Gingrich was elected six times after that. In the 1994 campaign season, in an effort to unite the Republican party further with the "Contract with America," it laid out ten policies with issues such as welfare reform, balanced budget, term limits, tougher crime laws, and even restrictions on the US participation in the United Nations. In 1994 the Republicans gained fifty-four seats and took control of the House for the first time since 1954. *Time Magazine* named Newt 1995 "Man of the Year" for his part in the election. As good as 1994 was for Republicans, 1998 was the reverse, losing five seats and losing the Senate. Gingrich announced his retirement from Congress and relinquished his speakership. His final remarks were that he was "not willing to preside over people who were cannibals."

Gingrich is still very involved in politics and governance. He is a member of the Council on Foreign Relations, a fellow at the American Enterprise Institute and Hoover Institution commentator, guest and panel member on cable news shows—specifically Fox News Channel. In 2010 his net worth was disclosed as $6.7 million; however, after speaking engagements at $60,000 per appearance and two successful books, that estimate has climbed to well over $20 million. Gingrich has been married three times and had one reported affair while he was married. He left his wife, Jackie Gingrich Cushman, and continued an affair with Marianne Ginther, and they were wed in 1981. That marriage lasted until 2000. Gingrich divorced Marianne and married Callista Bisek four months after his divorce; she is twenty-one years his junior. Gingrich has flip-flopped on his choice of religious faith. He was raised as a Lutheran, was a Southern Baptist while in graduate school, and then became a Catholic in 2008. The Catholic Church recognizes his third marriage as his only valid marriage. The first two marriages have been annulled by the church. Gingrich has written over thirty books and produced one film. He remains firmly in the media spotlight. Over the course of the 2016 campaign and currently, Gingrich has encouraged his fellow Republicans to unify behind Trump. Gingrich has tremendous clout with conservatives, and his ongoing endorsement of Trump will continue to help the POTUS base of supporters.

The Fox News and Fox Business News team has, in part, shown strong allegiance to Trump. Below is a Fox News list of those who support Trump and his views.

1. Sean Hannity
2. Tucker Carlson
3. Jessie Watters
4. Lou Dobbs
5. Judge Jeanine Pirro
6. Geraldo Rivera
7. Greg Gutfeld
8. Neal Cavuto
9. Nigel Farage
10. Steve Hilton
11. Oliver North
12. Stewart Varney
13. Andrew Napolitano
14. Harris Faulkner
15. Charles Payne
16. Charlie Gasparino
17. Michael Huckabee
18. Newt Gingrich
19. Eric Bowling
20. Lisa Boothe
21. Kimberly Guilfoyle
22. Laura Ingram
23. Chris Steigerwald

Not all the Fox News team is on board with Donald Trump. Some are even "Never Trumpers." I have compiled a list below of those who are neutral or

Never Trumpers. Note that N stands for neutral, and NT stands for Never Trump:

1. Shepard Smith—NT
2. Chris Wallace—NT
3. Juan Williams—NT
4. Joe Trippi—NT
5. Patrick Caddell—NT
6. Austin Goulsby—NT
7. John Roberts—NT
8. Britt Hume—NT
9. John Scott—N
10. Bill Hemmer—N
11. Ed Henry—N
12. Fred Barnes—N
13. Charles Krauthammer—N

Some of the Fox News team names were not included on the above list because evidence is not conclusive on which way they lean. The other news services, like CNN, MSNBC, ABC, CBS, NBC, and Univision, are not even mentioned as supporters of Trump because at least 95 percent would be Never Trump. The MSM list is either void of any names or just too few to mention.

Given the challenges that America faces and the fact that 95 percent of the media disagrees with Donald Trump all the time, along with weak leaders in Congress and the Senate, one would ask: How can Trump succeed in making America great? The answer to this question must be: Who around him stepped up to plate to fight with Trump? I think at this point, running the country as president of the United States is a team sport. With Donald Trump it is a team contact sport! The leader of the team has to have his or her team members by his or her side in support. That is the only way to win the game, and the only way America prevails and continues to dominate on the world stage is to have a team. The members of Congress and the Senate are void of competence. Remember the old sports saying about an athlete: "I don't think he can walk and chew gum at the same time"? I wonder if that is where we are at today. Can Congress show us that they have any ability at all to make changes? Do they even possess the talent? It does not appear to be the case. What happened to the "best and brightest"? They have not gone to Washington, DC, that is for sure—at least in recent years. How can we get good government back in America? What do we need to do as citizens of this great country? I asked the same important question in a previous book I wrote back in 2000, titled *Charity Is a Contact Sport*. In that publication, I gave a list of maybes:

Maybe—We will cure cancer.

Maybe—We will win the war on drugs and addiction.

Maybe—Poverty and hunger can be abated forever.

Maybe—We will stop gang and domestic violence.

Maybe—We can keep thousands of fish, wildlife, and forests from extinction.

Maybe—We can make school a better learning place.

Maybe—We can stop all racism and bigotry.

Maybe—We can get all religions to respect each other without interference and avarice.

Maybe—We can live with healthy family values that teach truth, faith, justice, and equality.

Maybe—We can have world peace.

Maybe…All of these hopes and goals listed above should not be listed as maybes. How about this: just ordinary people focused on making a difference can accomplish all these goals. Shame on us if we don't try to solve and provide these resources for every need listed above. Who gave the most when the giving was done? (In this case, who is going to step up to contribute to our society and great republic?) The answer is, "There was more than one."

EPILOGUE

In the end, and after all the controversy, the last 2016 POTUS election was not about Democrats versus Republicans; it was really about two candidates running against each other as the lesser of two evils. This is why the country became as divided as it is today. It is partly because both candidates were not considered the best America could offer. Neither would be greatly respected, because of his or her flaws; in fact, there was tremendous distrust, and the biggest question was: Who is worse, Trump or Hillary? So it came down to this: we all had to choose. The choice was one of the candidates with very "low" credibility, Donald Trump, and the other candidate with "no" credibility, Hillary Clinton. Why do I say Hillary had no credibility? Basically, it was around 38,000 reasons. Hillary erased 38,000 e-mails and never admitted to doing it. She had been caught in the act and denied any wrongdoing. Déjà vu with Bill Clinton and Monica Lewinski regarding the denial. Also she lost because Hillary was running for POTUS with forty years of Clinton family baggage. In the end I believe the Clinton family legacy and Hillary's numerous missteps showed the voters she was not prepared to be responsible and would not care or work hard enough to lead America. The "Crooked Hillary" nickname stuck with the voters. She also appeared more entitled than Trump in her attitude and demeanor. This attitude came out and was showing during the debates against Trump. Trump got the best of her, and the MSM kept protecting her from reality. The media and the polls gave her a false sense of security, along with the members of her campaign. I truly believe she felt that winning the election was in the bag. She had the "glass ceiling" of the first woman to be president. Trump spoke more directly to the people as a nonpolitician. He used words like liberty, safety, and prosperity exclusively and much more so than Clinton. Clinton stuck to the Democratic script of having the government to provide everything, and her presidency will fulfill your personal needs, so you can have more than you have today.

The impact that the United States has on the rest of the world has no boundaries. When Trump and his administration can focus on "America First," then they are correct in achieving that goal. American values and strength is what is needed first in the United States and must be reestablished in order for America to be the positive leader and protector of the rest of the world. The message to the rest of the world is this: "America can't help the rest of the world until it has its own house in order." Abraham Lincoln's famous quote, "A house divided cannot stand." America is divided now more so than anytime I can remember. So I say to all Americans, and to you, if you are a true American: Quit the bickering, stop the name-calling, and get on the same page so we can make a difference, not only for our lives but for the lives of our children and the future generations.

Trump is a political amateur, and this has shown to be the case, not only with himself but also with many of his White House staff. As a result, Trump has suffered numerous public-relations setbacks and been an open target of critical attacks from all sides, and not surprisingly, from his own party, the Republicans. There are Republicans who did not want Trump to rock the boat. These Republicans have their own agenda; that agenda is self-serving to them and their power base. Trump is considered an outsider and a disrupter. Consequently, Trump has used his friends and family members to help him with success in office. You can't blame him, because who can you really trust in Washington, DC, anymore? Trump's White House choices have not been the most experienced in government affairs, but they are professionals with strong educational and experienced business backgrounds. I believe in the end, this is the advantage that Trump has. He has the focus and leadership to accomplish more than any other president has accomplished in decades. The country was tired, when they voted in 2016, of one more politician in the White House. I will end this book with one last quote from me: "The ark was built by amateurs. The *Titanic* was built by professionals." Washington, DC, is a swamp. Perhaps Trump will not drain that swamp, but he can use his ark to float on top of the swamp. America needs that ark. If Hillary Clinton had won the 2016 election, we would all be on the *Titanic* right now, looking at an iceberg straight ahead over the bow!

Hillary is now POTUS history, and the Democrats have no message to deliver now or even in the near future. I am sure whoever the Democrats select for the 2020 nomination for president of the United States will put up a good fight and a good showing, but in the end Trump will win again in 2020. Nothing is set in stone, not in this day and age, but this "Trump Train" keeps on rolling along. The telltale benchmark will be the 2018 midterms, which will start the stage for the 2020 elections. In 2018 the Russia story will still be rolling along, because it will not stop until the Democrats decide to drop it. This will be the largest single mistake the Democrats have made in forty years, and I predict that keeping this story alive will almost wipe out the Democratic party as we know it. The Democrats will use the Russia story over and over again to attack the Republican candidates. This is the only issue the Democrats are running on, which is a weak Russia story and a story that will never prove an outright Trump collusion. It will not prove that the Russians aided Trump to win the election with specific help. All this will backfire in the end, because the American public no longer wishes to hear it. People in America are just fed up. Americans asked for positive changes and a new American dream; all they got from Democrats was *Russia*! The only person who can emerge to beat Trump will have to be someone who comes up with an entirely new message for America. The Democrats have suffered from a lack of decisiveness and having a positive message. Who knows if that new and exciting, bold candidate to unseat Trump is even out there? I don't see anyone as a current Democratic candidate or an independent candidate who has the courage of conviction, fortitude, confidence, speaking ability, and communication skills, much less the bold ideas, to match Trump. Common sense should rule the day, and Americans will see that it is we that hold the power and the resources to make a difference. If we attempt to rely on any government, local, state, or federal, we will always fall short and be sorely disappointed.

Made in the USA
San Bernardino, CA
31 March 2019